UNITED NATIONS CONFERENCE ON TRADE AND DEVELOPMENT

UNCTAD

ECONOMIC DEVELOPMENT IN AFRICA REPORT 2015

UNLOCKING THE POTENTIAL OF AFRICA'S SERVICES TRADE FOR GROWTH AND DEVELOPMENT

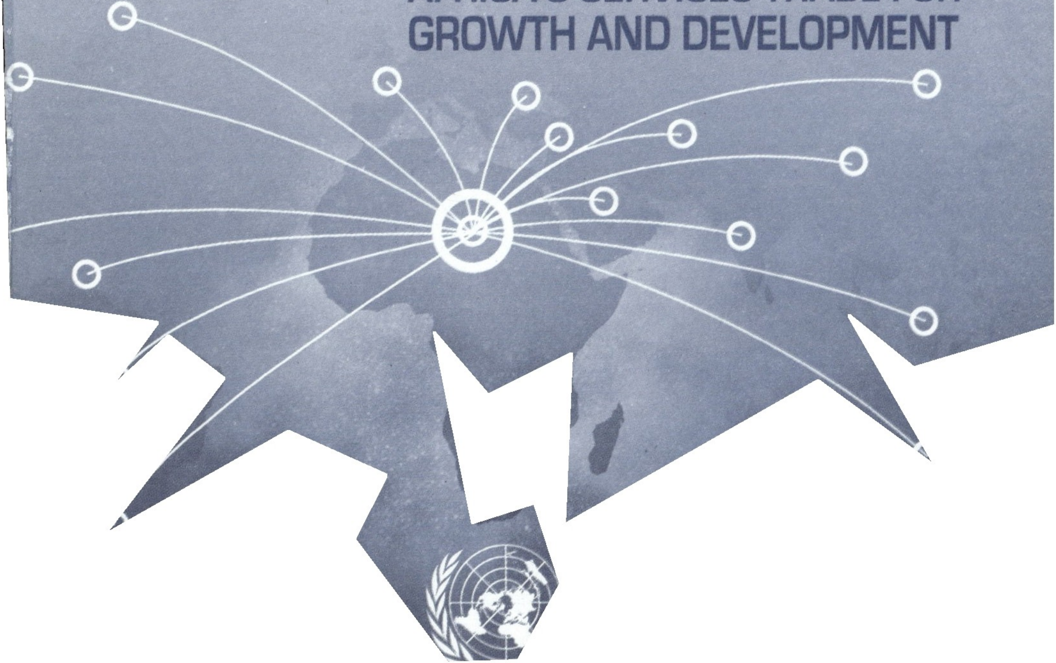

NOTE

Symbols of United Nations documents are composed of capital letters combined with figures. Mention of such a symbol indicates a reference to a United Nations document.

The designations employed and the presentation of the material do not imply the expression of any opinion on the part of the United Nations concerning the legal status of any country, territory, city or area, or of authorities or concerning the delimitation of its frontiers or boundaries.

Material in this publication may be freely quoted or reprinted, but acknowledgement is requested, together with a copy of the publication containing the quotation or reprint to be sent to the UNCTAD secretariat.

UNCTAD/ALDC/AFRICA/2015

UNITED NATIONS PUBLICATION
Sales No. E.15.II.D.2
ISBN 978-92-1-112888-8
eISBN 978-92-1-057284-2
ISSN 1990-5114

ACKNOWLEDGEMENTS

The *Economic Development in Africa Report 2015* was prepared by a team of UNCTAD contributors: Junior Roy Davis (team leader), Laura Páez and Bineswaree Bolaky. The work was completed under the overall supervision of Taffere Tesfachew, Director of the Division for Africa, Least Developed Countries and Special Programmes at UNCTAD.

An ad hoc expert group meeting on unlocking the potential of African services trade was held in Geneva on 21–22 January 2015 to conduct a peer review of the report. The meeting brought together specialists in the fields of services trade, finance, economic development and trade policy in Africa. The participants at the meeting were David Luke, Coordinator, African Trade Policy Centre, United Nations Economic Commission for Africa; Jane Drake-Brockman, Senior Services Adviser, International Trade Centre; Stephen Gelb, Director, World Trade Institute; and Vinaye Dey Ancharaz, Senior Development Economist, International Centre for Trade and Sustainable Development. Also participating were members of the *Economic Development in Africa Report* team. The following UNCTAD staff members also participated in the meeting and/or made comments on the draft: Lisa Borgatti, Mussie Delelegn, Sara Emanuelsson, Masataka Fujita, Samuel Gayi, Jan Hoffmann, Martine Julsaint Kidane, Joachim Karl, Benjamin McCarthy, Ahmad Mukhtar, Patrick Nwokedi Osakwe, Claudia Roethlisberger, Amelia Santos-Paulino, Rolf Traeger, Pamela Ugaz, Guillermo Valles, David Woodward, Anida Yupari and Liping Zhang.

Statistical assistance was provided by Agnès Collardeau-Angleys and Sanja Blazevic. Maria Bovey provided secretarial support. Sophie Combette designed the cover. Maritza Ascencios, Deniz Barki and Lucy Deleze-Black edited the report.

Madasamyraja Rajalingam did the overall layout, graphics and desktop publishing.

TABLES

EXPLANATORY NOTES

The $ sign refers to the United States dollar.

Sub-Saharan Africa: Except where otherwise stated, this includes South Africa.

North Africa: In this publication, the Sudan is classified as part of sub-Saharan Africa, not North Africa.

A hyphen (-) indicates that the data are either not available or not applicable.

ABBREVIATIONS

CEMAC	Communauté économique et monétaire de l'Afrique centrale
CFTA	continental free trade area
COMESA	Common Market for Eastern and Southern Africa
EAC	East African Community
ECOWAS	Economic Community of West African States
FDI	foreign direct investment
GATS	General Agreement on Trade in Services
GATT	General Agreement on Tariffs and Trade
GDP	gross domestic product
ICT	information and communications technology
IMF	International Monetary Fund
LDC	least developed country
M&A	mergers and acquisitions
MFN	most favoured nation
OECD	Organization for Economic Cooperation and Development
SADC	Southern African Development Community
SMEs	small and medium-sized enterprises

INTRODUCTION

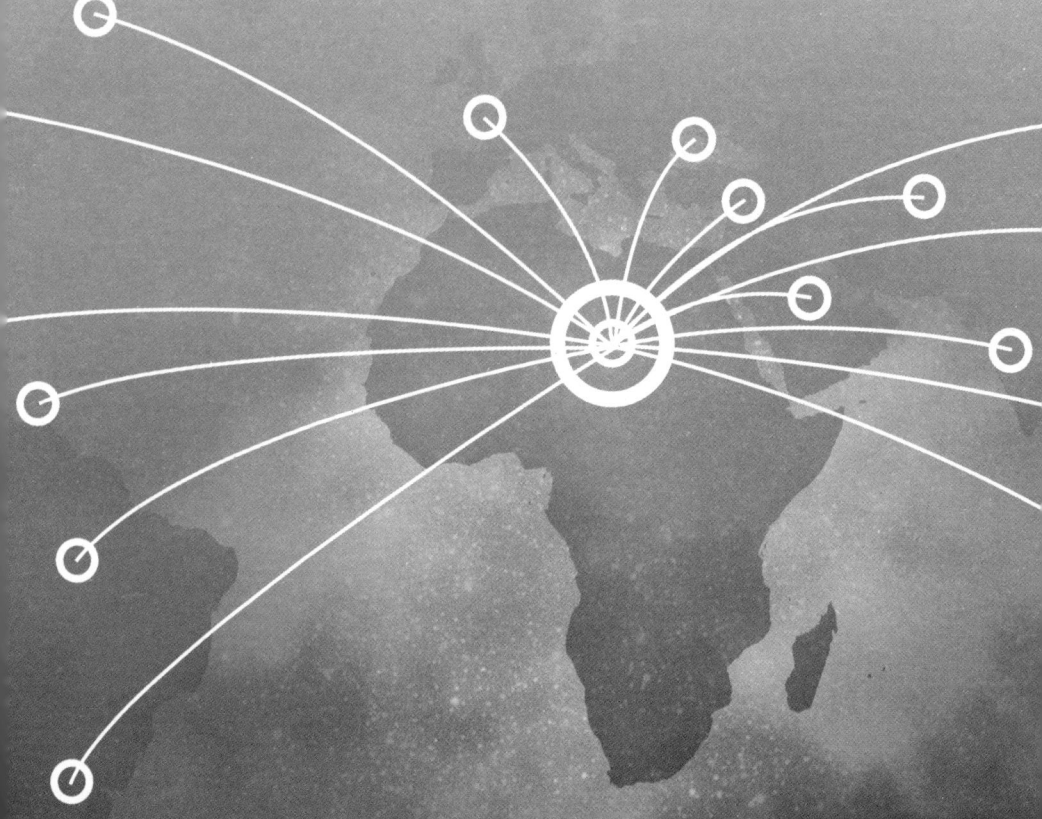

A. AFRICA'S SERVICES ECONOMY AND WHY IT MATTERS FOR THE CONTINENT

Africa's services sector holds tremendous economic promise. It contributes to almost half of the continent's output, and a number of African countries have emerged as services-oriented economies. Indeed, growth in services has been vibrant in Africa, at more than twice the average rate for the world during 2009–2012. The sector's performance has undoubtedly contributed to Africa's growth trajectory of the past decade.

The services economy in Africa is a vital source of income and employment. In some countries, as much as two thirds of the workforce is engaged in services. Overall, the services sector in Africa accounted for one third of formal employment during 2009–2012. If the informal sector were included, the relevance of services would be even greater. Furthermore, as Africa's middle class continues to grow, and given current population and urbanization trends (Africa's population is forecast to double by 2025), this sector is expected to expand.

Equally important is the sector's contribution to Africa's trade. African services exports and imports totalled $271 billion in 2012. Though Africa is a marginal player in global services trade, with an export share of only 2.2 per cent, the services sector represents an important source of export revenue that should be further exploited if Africa is to assume a role as a global player in services trade.

Services also have a vital role to play in the context of Africa's development strategy, whether it is based on the exploitation of its natural resource base (African Development Bank et al., 2013) or on labour-intensive light industry and manufacturing (Harrison et al., 2014; Lin and Rosenblatt, 2012). For either approach to succeed, exploiting the services potential of Africa will be critical to sustainable development. Indeed, as the most dominant sector in many African economies, services need to support the process of structural transformation, characterized by a shift from low- to high-productivity activities, and a declining share of agriculture in output and employment, as well as an increasing share of manufacturing and modern services in output. There are some dynamic emerging subsectors within the services sector with the potential to generate growth, trade and employment opportunities, which have yet to be tapped. For instance, logistics and distribution could greatly benefit Africa's agriculture (including agribusiness and food trade) and manufacturing sectors. Therefore, African policymakers need to place greater emphasis on how to move towards the provision of more sophisticated services where there is greater value addition and which offer opportunities for technology transfer and linkage development with other sectors of the economy.

Some services sectors are also considered to be the backbone of economic activity and have a bearing on social development. In particular, infrastructure services — encompassing transport, telecommunications, water, energy and financial services — are of critical importance to economic development and could contribute to addressing Africa's physical infrastructure deficit, inclusive growth and better social welfare. Infrastructure services also provide and support basic services (i.e. electricity, gas and potable water), which will be critical to the achievement of future post-2015 sustainable development goals. Lastly, infrastructure services are essential to the development of other service sectors, including tourism, distribution (wholesale, retail), information and communications technology (ICT) services, and business process outsourcing services. For infrastructure services to contribute successfully to the economic and social development of Africa, the institutional and regulatory environment must be supportive.

The continent is already tapping into some of the opportunities the services sector has to offer. For example, some African economies have been developing their services industries with relative success and are supplying services across Africa. Known examples of emerging regional services are the financial and banking services industries of Mauritius and Nigeria, the commercial and cargo air transport industry in Ethiopia and South Africa, the educational services industries of Uganda and Ghana, the telecommunication services of Egypt and the port services industries of Djibouti and Kenya.

Major challenges persist, however, especially as Africa seeks to move away from consumption-based growth to more durable sources of growth. The continent will need to shift away from relying on subsistence and non-tradable services to services which generate greater value addition and growth. Therefore, a key policy question is how to translate this services-led growth into sustainable employment and inclusive development for Africa.

B. MAIN FOCUS AND MESSAGES OF THE REPORT

Africa finds itself at an important crossroads in terms of defining and shaping its transformational agenda. The services sector can and must form part of this process, given the role it plays in Africa's economy. The Economic Development in Africa Report 2015 examines some of the major policy issues that underlie the continent's services sector and provides policy guidance on how services could contribute to regional integration in Africa and generate inclusive growth and employment. It analyses Africa's services sectors' regulatory and institutional frameworks, liberalization and growth at the regional level, and how services trade agreements and regulations (for example, the General Agreement on Trade in Services (GATS) and a continental free trade area (CFTA)) interface with the domestic regulation of services. Some of the key questions addressed in this report are as follows:

- What is the contribution of the services sector to the African economy and trade?

- How might the domestic regulatory and institutional framework improve the provision of services and the sector's contribution to growth?

- What national and regional policies need to be in place in order for services to make an enhanced contribution to African economies?

- Is there a potential role for a pan-African approach to services development/ integration?

- What services negotiations agenda should African countries pursue in regional and global services negotiations/forums?

- How does the national and regional policy landscape look for services trade in Africa, and how can it be made use of?

The key messages of the report are outlined in the following paragraphs.

First, the services sector has the potential to become a significant driver of sustained economic growth and structural transformation in Africa. This would, however, require policies to be aligned to build complementarities between the services sector and other sectors of the economy especially manufacturing. Africa must make greater efforts to link these services and industries, that is, to prioritize those services that are relevant for a value chain that is strategically important to a certain country.

Second, services provision remains suboptimal and is delivered at a high cost. Various regulatory and policy shortcomings prevail, which explain these inefficiencies and impede Africa from fully capitalizing on its services sector potential. For Africa to better harness the potential of its services economy, regulation of and policies for infrastructure services need to better target existing market failures including issues of accessibility, quality, affordability and competition.

Third, although African countries have made efforts to address services trade at the national, regional and global levels, a policy disconnect prevails between these three levels, hampering Africa's opportunities to tap into the benefits of greater services trade.

Lastly, the report makes specific and actionable policy recommendations on how to better harness the potential of Africa's services trade and the related development, employment and growth benefits.

C. ORGANIZATION OF THE REPORT

The report is organized in five chapters. Chapter 1 provides empirical evidence on economic trends in the services sector and the sector's actual contribution to African economies. Chapter 2 examines the economic development potential of the regulation of infrastructure, whether public or privately owned, to boost growth and regional integration in Africa. Chapter 3 evaluates the existing policies that pertain to the services sector at the national, regional and global levels, in an effort to define how well such policies target the sector and the sector's contribution to development goals of African Governments, such as the CFTA. Chapter 4 focuses solely on the banking and financial services sector in Africa and examines cross-border expansion, financial inclusion, product innovation and regulation.

On the basis of the previous analysis, chapter 5 provides an outline of the main policy findings on services trade. It also highlights the lessons learned from the experiences and best practices discussed in chapters 1 to 4.

CHAPTER **1**

THE SERVICES SECTOR
IN AFRICA:
EMERGING TRENDS

A. INTRODUCTION

In many African countries, the services sector constitutes the largest segment of the economy, and during the period 2000–2012, the sector contributed an increasing share to gross domestic product (GDP), trade and employment. The development of efficient and competitive services economies and trade, especially in infrastructure services such as telecommunications, transport, energy and finance, could significantly improve the economic outlook in Africa.

This chapter outlines key stylized facts about the services sector in Africa, based on both national and international sources of data. These facts capture the importance of the services sector in African national economies in terms of their contribution to GDP, trade and employment, and highlight areas for boosting the potential of services in Africa. Box 1 summarizes selected conceptual issues concerning the definition, classification and treatment of services data in economic analysis.

B. STYLIZED FACTS ON THE SERVICES SECTOR IN AFRICA

From the period 2001–2004 to the period 2009–2012, the share of services in African output rose from 45.8 to 49 per cent. The share of services in real output was highest among exporters of manufactured goods.

Table 1 shows the distribution of total value added in Africa (in constant 2005 dollars) by sector.[1] The share of services in Africa's real output rose from 45.8 to 49.0 per cent from the period 2001–2004 to the period 2009–2012. This mirrored the trend in developing economies, where the share of services in real output rose from 51.9 to 52.8 per cent over the same period. In Africa, the share of services in real output was highest among exporters of manufactured goods (comprising Lesotho and Tunisia), at 61.7 per cent, followed by services exporters at 57.0 per cent, and lowest among fuel exporters, at 33.9 per cent. This may indicate that services are an important determinant of competitiveness in manufacturing exports.

Within the services sector in Africa, during the period 2009–2012, the shares of subsectors were as follows: wholesale trade, retail trade, restaurants and hotels accounted for 14.5 per cent of output; transport, storage and communications accounted for 9.2 per cent of output; and other activities accounted for 25.2 per cent of output. The shares of these services categories in total services in Africa also mirrored the shares observed in developing economies.

The wholesale trade, retail trade, restaurants and hotels subsector contributed more than 25 per cent to output in the Gambia and Sao Tome and Principe during the period 2009–2012. The transport, storage and communications subsector accounted for more than 25 per cent of output only in Djibouti, a major services exporter, reflecting the economic importance of its port services to neighbouring landlocked countries and its strategic location close to the Suez Canal. The other activities category represented more than 40 per cent of output in Lesotho, Namibia, South Africa and Seychelles.

In countries where the services sector is already a major contributor to GDP and exports, an important policy question is how to use the sector as a launch pad for creating further employment and delivering on inclusive growth and sustainable development. This requires understanding the constraints of the sector in order to enhance its competitiveness, as well as identifying opportunities for optimizing backward and forward linkages between the services sector and other sectors that have a potential for growth and are critical for economic development.

During the period 2009–2012, 21 African countries had a share of services in output greater than 50 per cent.

As shown in table 1, during the period 2009–2012, the share of services in real output accounted for more than 50 per cent on average in 21 African countries (excluding South Sudan). Seychelles was the most services-dominant economy (80 per cent), followed by Djibouti, Mauritius and South Africa. However, of the 21 countries, only the following eight — mostly relatively small countries dependent on travel and tourism services — were dependent on the exports of services: Cabo Verde; Djibouti; the Gambia; Madagascar; Mauritius; Rwanda; Sao Tome and Principe; and Seychelles. In most African countries where the share of services in real output was above 50 per cent, the services sector was mostly domestic demand-driven rather than exports-led. Although the Comoros, Ethiopia and Liberia were classified as services exports-dependent during the period 2009–2012, the share of services in output in these countries did not exceed 50 per cent.

The least services-dependent economies were Equatorial Guinea, Liberia, Angola, the Congo, Chad and Libya, all of which, with the exception of Liberia, are among the top eight oil-exporting economies in Africa. Equatorial Guinea was the only country with a share of services in output of less than 5 per cent. From the

Table 1. Distribution of real total value added by sector and country, 2001–2012 (Percentage)

Exports specialization	Agriculture, hunting, forestry and fishing 2001–2004	2009–2012	Industry 2001–2004	2009–2012	Mining, manufacturing and utilities 2001–2004	2009–2012	Manufacturing 2001–2004	2009–2012	Construction 2001–2004	2009–2012	Services 2001–2004	2009–2012	Wholesale trade, retail trade, restaurants and hotels 2001–2004	2009–2012	Transport, storage and communications 2001–2004	2009–2012	Other activities 2001–2004	2009–2012
Food and agriculture	*41*	*39*	*15*	*18*	*12*	*15*	*10*	*13*	*3*	*3*	*43*	*46*	*14*	*16*	*7*	*8*	*23*	*23*
Côte d'Ivoire	25	26	24	18	21	16	16	12	2	2	51	59	12	13	8	9	32	36
Guinea-Bissau	42	43	16	14	14	12	13	11	2	2	42	44	21	21	4	5	17	17
Malawi	37	26	14	32	10	27	8	25	3	5	48	50	13	20	6	6	30	24
Somalia	62	60	7	7	3	3	2	2	4	4	31	32	10	11	9	10	12	12
Fuels	*14*	*13*	*60*	*52*	*57*	*46*	*4*	*5*	*3*	*3*	*25*	*34*	*10*	*12*	*5*	*7*	*11*	*14*
Algeria	8	10	60	50	53	41	4	5	3	5	32	41	10	14	8	7	14	16
Angola	8	9	71	65	67	59	4	5	7	10	21	23	11	14	3	5	7	16
Chad	29	22	31	41	30	40	8	6	1	1	30	30	14	14	2	2	14	13
Congo	5	4	74	70	71	67	8	5	3	4	22	23	6	7	4	5	11	11
Equatorial Guinea	3	1	96	89	94	85	0	0	1	4	3	3	1	1	0	0	2	3
Gabon	4	4	61	55	59	52	4	6	2	3	35	39	15	17	6	6	14	15
Libya	2	2	76	63	72	58	5	4	2	2	22	30	3	5	3	6	15	20
Nigeria	32	32	47	32	46	30	3	3	..	..	22	31	11	18	2	6	9	8
South Sudan	..	9	..	27	..	12	..	5	..	15	..	76	..	16	..	20	..	39
Sudan	38	34	20	24	16	19	8	8	4	5	43	43	16	15	12	13	15	15
Manufactured goods	*10*	*9*	*31*	*30*	*25*	*25*	*19*	*17*	*6*	*5*	*58*	*62*	*12*	*11*	*8*	*12*	*38*	*39*
Lesotho	10	8	32	34	26	28	20	17	6	6	58	58	8	9	5	9	44	41
Tunisia	10	9	30	26	25	21	18	16	5	5	59	65	15	14	11	15	33	36
Mixed exporters	*27*	*26*	*24*	*24*	*19*	*18*	*13*	*11*	*4*	*6*	*49*	*51*	*15*	*15*	*8*	*9*	*27*	*26*
Benin	36	35	14	14	10	9	9	8	5	5	49	51	18	18	8	7	23	24
Burkina Faso	39	40	17	16	12	11	11	6	3	5	44	44	11	15	5	5	28	24
Burundi	43	38	17	15	14	11	12	9	3	4	40	47	19	21	3	5	18	21
Cameroon	20	22	35	28	32	24	19	17	4	3	46	49	22	22	5	5	19	20
Central African Republic	54	53	14	15	12	10	6	7	4	4	32	50	12	13	4	8	15	12
Egypt	15	13	37	39	33	33	17	6	4	6	48	60	14	15	10	12	23	21
Eritrea	14	17	23	23	12	8	10	9	11	16	64	49	21	19	13	16	30	28
Ghana	32	27	20	24	15	16	11	12	5	9	48	58	11	11	15	8	21	22
Kenya	27	23	19	25	21	14	12	14	6	5	54	59	14	14	11	8	32	30
Morocco	15	16	27	22	20	18	16	13	6	7	58	51	11	13	6	13	37	38
Mozambique	28	27	24	27	25	19	15	14	3	3	49	51	14	16	11	13	24	22
Namibia	12	7	28	27	25	23	13	14	3	4	60	65	13	15	5	7	42	43
Niger	45	48	12	12	10	10	6	6	2	3	43	40	15	14	7	6	21	19

Table 1 (continued)

Exports specialization	Agriculture, hunting, forestry and fishing		Industry		Mining, manufacturing and utilities		Manufacturing		Construction		Services		Wholesale trade, retail trade, restaurants and hotels		Transport, storage and communications		Other activities	
	2001–2004	2009–2012	2001–2004	2009–2012	2001–2004	2009–2012	2001–2004	2009–2012	2001–2004	2009–2012	2001–2004	2009–2012	2001–2004	2009–2012	2001–2004	2009–2012	2001–2004	2009–2012
Senegal	17	16	24	23	20	18	16	14	4	5	59	61	22	20	9	14	28	27
Sierra Leone	49	52	11	15	9	13	3	2	2	2	40	34	9	8	6	7	25	18
South Africa	3	3	32	28	29	25	19	17	2	3	66	69	14	14	10	10	42	45
Swaziland	9	8	45	38	41	35	39	33	4	3	47	54	11	14	5	8	31	32
Togo	45	41	19	19	16	14	10	10	2	5	37	42	11	9	5	6	21	27
Uganda	29	19	22	25	12	11	7	7	10	14	50	54	18	19	5	8	27	27
United Rep. of Tanzania	33	27	21	24	13	14	8	9	8	10	46	49	15	16	6	8	24	25
Zimbabwe	13	10	38	46	38	46	6	7	0	0	47	46	17	13	3	4	27	30
Ores and metals	29	25	30	28	24	21	8	7	6	8	41	46	15	17	4	7	21	21
Botswana	2	2	48	33	42	25	6	8	6	8	50	66	13	21	4	6	34	39
Democratic Rep. of the Congo	55	44	19	23	16	18	5	5	3	5	28	31	16	19	3	4	9	8
Guinea	23	20	33	34	25	27	6	7	8	4	40	44	18	18	6	8	15	18
Mali	38	41	25	19	20	15	9	6	5	4	38	39	14	16	4	6	20	17
Mauritania	33	26	30	31	26	25	10	5	4	6	37	44	8	8	5	13	24	22
Zambia	24	19	25	30	17	16	11	10	8	14	52	49	22	18	4	7	25	24
Services	29	25	16	18	11	11	8	7	6	7	55	57	17	18	12	14	25	25
Cabo Verde	14	10	22	24	12	12	6	6	10	12	64	66	15	17	19	19	30	31
Comoros	49	49	12	10	6	5	4	4	6	5	39	41	18	17	5	8	17	15
Djibouti	3	4	15	19	8	9	3	3	6	10	81	77	20	22	27	27	35	28
Ethiopia	46	40	13	13	8	8	5	5	5	5	41	48	15	18	5	5	22	25
Gambia	27	26	14	14	8	10	6	6	5	4	59	60	34	27	11	14	15	19
Liberia	77	61	6	16	4	14	3	6	2	3	17	17	4	5	5	6	8	7
Madagascar	29	28	18	20	16	15	14	13	2	4	53	52	11	11	19	19	23	22
Mauritius	6	5	29	25	24	19	22	17	6	6	64	70	18	18	11	13	35	38
Rwanda	44	34	14	16	8	7	7	7	6	9	41	50	12	17	6	9	23	24
Sao Tome and Principe	20	18	18	17	10	10	11	7	8	8	63	65	25	26	14	17	25	22
Seychelles	4	2	18	18	13	10	11	7	5	8	78	80	20	20	15	16	43	44
Developing economies	10	8	38	39	33	33	14	22	6	6	52	53	14	15	8	8	30	30
Africa	16	16	39	35	35	29	12	11	4	5	46	49	13	14	8	8	25	25
America	6	5	34	32	28	25	17	16	6	7	60	63	16	17	8	10	36	36
Asia	11	8	40	42	34	35	13	26	5	6	49	50	13	14	7	8	29	29

Source: UNCTAD secretariat calculations, based on data from UNCTADStat, available at http://unctadstat/EN/index.html.
Notes: Averages are calculated based on years for which data are available for South Sudan, data are available only for 2012). Data are based on national systems of accounts and are presented according to six categories of exports specializations (food and agriculture, fuels, manufactured goods, mixed exporters, ores and metals and services). A country is classified under a given category if the share of exports in that category accounts for more than 45 per cent of total exports, based on values during the period 2009–2012. Mixed exporters are countries in which no single category accounts for more than 45 per cent of total exports. The sum of the shares of the three main economic sectors is not always 100 per cent due to discrepancies between total value added and the sum of value added across the three sectors in the original data and due to rounding.

period 2001–2004 to the period 2009–2012, the share of services in real output expanded in 45 countries. The expansion was most significant in Botswana, where the share of services in output over this period rose by 15.6 percentage points, from 50.3 to 65.9 per cent. The largest contraction was in Sierra Leone, a post-conflict country where the share of services in output fell from 40.3 per cent during the period 2001–2004 to 34.1 per cent during the period 2009–2012. The second largest contraction was in Djibouti, a major services exporter, where the share of services in output fell from 81.5 per cent during the period 2001–2004 to 77.2 per cent during the period 2009–2012, mainly due to the postponement of planned foreign direct investment (FDI) and a reduction in port operations, upon which the country's economy heavily depends.

During the periods 2001–2004 and 2009–2012, of the 45 countries where the share of services in output rose, 30 experienced a contraction in manufacturing.

Many African countries have undergone a process of shifting from agricultural to mainly non-tradable services, without undergoing a process of manufacturing development marked by significant productivity improvements, formal job creation, exports of sophisticated goods and the application of technology to the wider economy. Table 1 shows that during the periods 2001–2004 and 2009–2012, of the 45 countries where the share of services in output rose, 30 experienced a contraction in manufacturing. This suggests that the complementary elements between the two sectors have yet to be fully developed in some countries.

The services sector in Africa has a critical role to play in the industrial and manufacturing development of African countries, as well as in boosting agricultural productivity. Africa needs to raise investment in infrastructure, encompassing a range of services subsectors, in order to achieve its development goals of structural transformation and economic diversification (UNCTAD, 2014a). Building complementarity, that is, strengthening input–output and demand linkages between services, manufacturing and agriculture remains a necessary continental goal.

Africa's services sector grew at more than twice the world average rate during the period 2009–2012.

During the period 2009–2012, the services sector grew rapidly in real terms in Africa, at more than twice the world average rate (see table 2). Growth was particularly strong in Eastern and Western Africa.

During this period, the services sector in Africa grew at a rate of 4.6 per cent, compared to 5.4 per cent in the developing world. The wholesale trade, retail trade, restaurants and hotels category grew at 5.0 per cent, compared to 5.8 per cent for the transport, storage and communications category and 4.0 per cent for other activities. Of the 10 countries (Burundi, Chad, the Congo, Côte d'Ivoire, Equatorial Guinea, Ethiopia, Ghana, Nigeria, Rwanda and Togo) where the services sector grew fastest in real terms during this period, at an annual average rate of more than 8 per cent, only Ethiopia and Rwanda were services exports-dependent. In the services exports-dependent economies of Cabo Verde, the Comoros, Mauritius, Sao Tome and Principe and Seychelles, services growth was below the African average of 4.6 per cent, reflecting a potential slowing down of the services sector in these countries. Furthermore, in the 53 African countries considered in this analysis, there was an estimated inverse correlation between the share of services in GDP during the same period and real growth in the services sector (a negative correlation coefficient of -0.27), which suggests that growth was fastest in countries that were among the least services-oriented and that some countries made significant progress in developing their services sector potential, albeit from a low base, for example Burundi and Equatorial Guinea.

Among the 10 fastest growing economies by services sector, four countries are major fuel exporters (Chad, the Congo, Equatorial Guinea and Nigeria). This may indicate a potential nexus between fuel exports revenues and services, with booming oil revenues supporting an increase in demand for services in some African economies. Averaging the real growth rate in services across categories of exports specializations shows that the real growth in services during the periods 2001–2004 and 2009–2012 was highest among fuel exporters (8.6 and 7.8 per cent, respectively) and lowest among food and agriculture exporters. Similarly, during the period 2009–2012, the manufacturing sector in all major fuel-exporting countries grew at a rate of 9.3 per cent on average, compared to 5.2 per cent for manufactured goods-exporting countries.

As shown in table 3, at the country level, during the period 2009–2012, the services sector grew at a double digit rate in Burundi, Equatorial Guinea, Ethiopia and Nigeria. The sector contracted only in Madagascar, a services exports-dependent country that experienced a major retrenchment in public investment, official development assistance receipts and tourism, due to significant political turmoil during the period 2009–2011 (Ploch and Cook, 2012).

Table 2. Growth in real gross domestic product and services and its components by region, 2001–2012 (Percentage)

Group	Gross domestic product		Services		Wholesale trade, retail trade, restaurants and hotels		Transport, storage and communi- cations		Other activities	
	2001– 2004	2009– 2012	2001– 2004	2009– 2012	2001– 2004	2009– 2012	2001– 2004	2009– 2012	2001– 2004	2009– 2012
World	2.72	1.79	2.68	1.99	2.90	1.94	3.73	1.88	2.43	2.04
Developing economies	4.94	5.25	4.97	5.40	4.59	5.83	6.62	5.59	4.75	5.15
Developed economies	1.99	0.44	2.15	1.04	2.27	0.40	2.81	0.37	2.02	1.33
Developing economies: Africa	5.08	3.41	4.76	4.60	4.30	5.02	7.32	5.75	4.26	3.95
Eastern Africa	4.01	7.02	4.26	7.94	3.19	7.48	6.33	9.38	4.28	7.69
Middle Africa	6.87	4.42	5.91	5.03	6.60	4.65	7.24	5.40	4.65	5.45
Northern Africa	4.72	1.63	4.89	3.29	3.17	2.86	7.39	3.95	4.91	3.22
Southern Africa	3.51	1.97	4.11	2.83	3.05	3.04	6.51	2.31	3.94	2.88
Western Africa	8.29	6.27	6.31	9.05	8.44	9.23	10.19	14.15	3.46	6.22
Developing economies: America	2.15	2.88	2.21	3.35	1.77	3.06	3.13	3.99	2.21	3.34
Developing economies: Asia	6.14	6.29	6.41	6.30	6.09	7.02	8.19	6.18	6.11	5.99

Source: UNCTAD secretariat calculations, based on data from UNCTADStat.
Note: Figures relate to annual growth in value of GDP and services and its components at constant 2005 dollars, averaged over the given periods.

There has been vigorous growth in the telecommunications sector in Burundi, fuelled by FDI as a result of liberalization measures in the mobile telephony market introduced by the Government. Ethiopia has implemented a Promoting Basic Services Programme since 2012, to improve access to education, health, water and sanitation services by the poor and to improve its transport infrastructure to promote trade. The rebasing of Nigeria's national accounts in 2014 highlighted the emergence of new services subsectors, notably the electricity, gas, steam and air conditioning supply sectors, as well as the sound recording, film and music production industries (Mail and Guardian, 2014). There has also been a dramatic increase in the number of cellular telephone subscribers in Nigeria, since the Government issued cellular telephone licenses in 2002, and resurgent growth in the banking sector since central bank reforms increased capital requirements for banks, which led to significant consolidation in the industry (Mail and Guardian, 2014).

Table 3. Growth in real gross domestic product, services and exports of goods and services by country, 2001–2012 (Percentage)

Exports specialization	Gross domestic product		Services		Exports of goods and services	
	2001–2004	2009–2012	2001–2004	2009–2012	2001–2004	2009–2012
Food and agriculture						
Côte d'Ivoire	-0.42	2.52	-1.29	8.55	1.37	4.20
Guinea-Bissau	0.81	2.59	-0.71	2.46	-3.14	0.06
Malawi	2.48	2.89	3.42	0.47	14.61	2.09
Somalia	3.25	2.60	3.44	1.94	1.32	3.14
Fuels						
Algeria	5.02	2.62	4.92	5.21	3.40	-3.96
Angola	8.04	4.13	7.39	4.57	1.98	-4.00
Chad	17.00	7.05	9.00	9.51	45.89	-0.25
Congo	3.19	7.25	7.18	8.04	-2.41	0.47
Equatorial Guinea	33.81	2.62	21.25	12.11	22.14	-1.12
Gabon	0.70	4.60	1.60	4.36	-2.13	0.09
Libya	4.17	11.70	6.10	6.86	7.14	11.87
Nigeria	12.43	7.03	11.67	11.72	4.60	8.05
South Sudan	..	..	..	..	..	..
Sudan	7.34	4.61	7.51	2.45	9.69	2.39
Manufactured goods						
Lesotho	2.94	4.80	2.84	4.95	23.84	0.03
Tunisia	4.49	2.17	5.57	3.61	3.41	1.49
Mixed exporters						
Benin	4.42	3.53	4.06	3.41	1.86	2.08
Burkina Faso	5.81	5.68	7.50	7.86	3.54	26.19
Burundi	2.45	10.46	9.63	10.39	5.48	-1.77
Cameroon	4.06	3.66	7.30	4.21	1.77	-0.86
Central African Republic	-1.07	3.00	-5.04	3.41	-9.43	5.52
Egypt	3.49	3.45	3.76	4.01	7.69	-4.64
Eritrea	2.64	5.58	4.31	7.95	2.50	84.22
Ghana	4.98	8.73	5.06	8.73	-13.09	17.96
Kenya	3.26	4.37	3.16	5.02	7.65	4.86
Morocco	5.50	4.02	4.62	4.71	6.42	1.68
Mozambique	8.96	7.05	7.53	7.33	32.24	13.82
Namibia	5.62	3.70	5.02	5.10	6.95	0.40
Niger	3.84	5.20	2.49	4.52	-0.10	16.01

Table 3 (continued)

Exports specialization	GDP		Services		Exports of goods and services	
	2001–2004	2009–2012	2001–2004	2009–2012	2001–2004	2009–2012
Senegal	4.45	3.13	5.22	3.45	4.60	4.33
Sierra Leone	15.13	11.76	12.57	5.87	30.69	72.33
South Africa	3.48	1.89	4.12	2.58	1.58	-2.24
Swaziland	2.02	0.73	2.93	2.46	6.17	6.95
Togo	1.21	4.52	-2.99	9.82	5.20	12.87
Uganda	6.95	5.20	8.03	6.19	15.60	-2.54
United Republic of Tanzania	6.98	6.61	7.46	7.79	13.28	17.33
Zimbabwe	-4.31	10.38	-3.29	7.28	-22.85	62.33
Ores and metals						
Botswana	3.41	2.63	3.57	7.50	0.85	-0.28
Democratic Rep. of the Congo	3.45	6.00	3.80	5.52	38.33	5.99
Guinea	3.10	2.40	1.85	1.11	2.95	10.07
Mali	6.51	2.96	5.00	0.49	7.30	5.55
Mauritania	3.60	3.86	7.91	5.82	0.42	5.80
Zambia	4.67	7.04	4.32	6.05	28.41	12.13
Services						
Cabo Verde	5.10	2.38	5.79	2.94	-0.97	3.26
Comoros	2.43	1.91	1.61	1.91	0.39	2.04
Djibouti	2.70	4.50	2.16	4.97	4.89	14.00
Ethiopia	5.31	10.25	4.94	12.31	17.43	0.87
Gambia	4.44	3.68	0.84	5.30	-18.94	60.30
Liberia	-5.46	8.65	-0.83	7.95	2.35	7.93
Madagascar	2.10	0.11	1.40	-0.66	3.15	0.36
Mauritius	3.80	3.51	5.30	4.38	-0.18	5.17
Rwanda	7.38	7.42	8.73	9.07	25.66	15.65
Sao Tome and Principe	4.05	4.86	6.07	3.65	1.25	3.82
Seychelles	-2.33	3.32	-2.01	3.59	-2.21	-1.43
Developing economies	*5.33*	*5.25*	*5.41*	*5.40*	*8.68*	*4.36*
Africa	5.27	3.41	5.04	4.60	4.66	-0.48
America	2.62	2.88	2.77	3.35	5.08	2.78
Asia	6.51	6.29	6.78	6.30	10.04	5.11

Source: UNCTAD secretariat calculations, based on data from UNCTADStat.

Note: Figures relate to annual growth in value of GDP and services and exports of goods and services at constant 2005 dollars, averaged over the given periods.

Table 4 shows real growth in the services sector by category. Over the period 2009–2012, real growth exceeded 10 per cent in the wholesale trade, retail trade, restaurants and hotels subsector in countries such as Burkina Faso, Burundi, Chad, Ethiopia, Libya, Nigeria and Togo. Real growth exceeded 10 per cent in the transport, storage and communications subsector in 11 countries, including Burundi (26 per cent) and Nigeria (23 per cent). In the other activities category, growth exceeded 10 per cent only in Equatorial Guinea, Ethiopia and Togo.

Identifying the drivers of services growth in Africa requires understanding factors accounting for both an increase in demand for services and in supply. On the demand side, the growth of services is driven by broader economic growth, rising exports revenues and a growing population. As both disposable incomes and urbanization increase, the demand for infrastructure services also rise. During the period 2009–2012, simple correlation coefficients between growth in the services sector and real GDP growth was a high 0.63 and coefficients between services growth and growth in exports was 0.19. On the supply side, the services sector tends to expand as countries undertake commitments to improve access to basic services (for example as undertaken in Ethiopia) and reforms to introduce greater competition among services suppliers, and as regional integration deepens through projects to improve transport and logistics.

The services sector was the most important driver of growth in 30 out of 54 countries during the period 2009–2012.

Figure 1 shows the sharp expansion of the services sector in real terms in Africa since 2000, which was maintained during the 2008–2009 global crisis. The services sector can play an important role in cushioning the effect of global economic shocks in Africa, by sustaining domestic consumption and domestic output when exports are adversely affected by international crises.

Weighted real GDP growth rates were calculated for each African country and the contribution of the services sector to real growth was assessed.[2] The analysis reinforced the importance of services as a cushion for national economies at times of global economic shock. During the period 2009–2012, the services sector was the most significant driver of economic growth in 30 out of 54 countries, accounting for more than 50 per cent of real economic growth. The sector accounted for more than 70 per cent of total real economic growth in 12 countries, and in seven of these countries, services accounted for more than 50 per cent of GDP. In Côte d'Ivoire, Madagascar, Mali, Seychelles and Swaziland, the services sector accounted for

Table 4.   Real growth in services categories by country, 2001–2012 (Percentage)

Exports specialization	Wholesale trade, retail trade, restaurants and hotels		Transport, storage and communications		Other activities	
	2001–2004	2009–2012	2001–2004	2009–2012	2001–2004	2009–2012
Food and agriculture						
Côte d'Ivoire	-0.73	8.55	-1.07	8.56	-1.54	8.54
Guinea-Bissau	2.61	-0.27	4.25	4.36	-5.45	5.84
Malawi	4.61	4.71	8.40	2.41	2.12	-1.97
Somalia	3.55	1.93	3.31	1.93	3.46	1.94
Fuels						
Algeria	6.18	6.13	5.30	4.16	3.84	5.15
Angola	7.35	4.19	7.98	4.14	7.18	6.12
Chad	8.51	12.05	9.68	17.30	9.61	5.90
Congo	8.52	10.13	13.42	9.64	4.39	5.93
Equatorial Guinea	22.92	3.20	14.46	2.95	21.19	16.04
Gabon	2.08	4.17	-0.96	3.86	2.36	4.80
Libya	11.36	12.40	11.67	12.05	4.07	5.82
Nigeria	13.28	10.94	27.21	22.78	6.61	6.50
South Sudan	..	..	..	..	..	..
Sudan	2.76	3.57	13.27	2.21	8.82	1.62
Manufactured goods						
Lesotho	3.33	4.23	8.59	6.50	2.10	4.84
Tunisia	4.53	0.65	7.19	4.18	5.52	4.65
Mixed exporters						
Benin	3.62	2.05	4.37	5.43	4.30	3.74
Burkina Faso	6.84	12.38	9.91	5.62	7.75	6.25
Burundi	11.47	10.96	10.79	26.38	7.73	7.66
Cameroon	9.16	3.04	9.46	5.80	4.77	4.96
Central African Republic	-1.08	3.80	-1.39	4.30	-8.61	2.86
Egypt	0.09	3.49	5.94	5.67	5.45	3.39
Eritrea	4.83	7.94	4.82	7.94	3.75	7.96
Ghana	5.42	6.75	5.55	10.08	4.53	8.79
Kenya	3.31	6.98	8.35	5.24	1.64	4.03
Morocco	3.37	2.42	9.54	9.42	4.32	4.52
Mozambique	8.32	5.65	6.95	11.59	7.36	6.22
Namibia	6.31	5.78	12.23	4.23	3.82	5.01
Niger	3.59	3.96	4.31	6.04	1.10	4.43

Table 4 (continued)

Exports specialization	Wholesale trade, retail trade, restaurants and hotels		Transport, storage and communications		Other activities	
	2001–2004	2009–2012	2001–2004	2009–2012	2001–2004	2009–2012
Senegal	3.35	2.79	13.30	4.13	4.21	3.58
Sierra Leone	16.91	7.17	26.67	5.45	8.75	5.46
South Africa	3.06	2.66	6.54	2.09	3.93	2.67
Swaziland	-0.08	2.18	10.49	3.73	2.89	2.30
Togo	1.34	12.84	6.42	1.16	-6.81	11.59
Uganda	6.08	4.47	14.85	8.68	8.18	6.84
United Republic of Tanzania	6.91	7.49	7.66	12.03	7.74	6.63
Zimbabwe	-13.19	5.66	-1.36	5.21	3.62	8.39
Ores and metals						
Botswana	1.40	8.16	-1.29	9.35	5.03	6.92
Democratic Rep. of the Congo	2.54	6.03	17.04	5.80	2.20	4.32
Guinea	1.92	-0.52	1.68	1.84	1.85	2.74
Mali	6.11	3.74	6.72	3.03	3.97	-3.19
Mauritania	6.85	4.46	27.50	10.55	5.29	4.15
Zambia	5.89	4.07	3.95	12.25	3.05	5.91
Services						
Cabo Verde	9.39	3.39	3.61	2.15	5.63	3.24
Comoros	-1.81	1.91	18.25	1.91	1.49	1.91
Djibouti	4.16	5.52	2.35	5.87	0.96	3.73
Ethiopia	4.43	11.74	9.82	11.29	4.24	12.98
Gambia	-3.85	1.85	16.85	8.54	2.56	8.83
Liberia	1.80	7.95	8.49	7.95	-6.45	7.95
Madagascar	1.12	1.75	0.81	-1.01	2.23	-1.38
Mauritius	3.59	2.18	7.81	6.08	5.50	4.91
Rwanda	10.41	7.98	12.55	10.63	7.03	9.27
Sao Tome and Principe	6.75	3.33	8.52	3.87	4.19	3.88
Seychelles	-1.17	5.55	-5.23	2.11	-1.07	3.37
Developing economies	*5.27*	*5.83*	*6.95*	*5.59*	*5.10*	*5.15*
Africa	4.94	5.02	7.55	5.75	4.35	3.95
America	2.59	3.06	3.82	3.99	2.61	3.34
Asia	6.68	7.02	8.35	6.18	6.44	5.99

Source: UNCTAD secretariat calculations, based on data from UNCTADStat.
Note: Figures relate to annual growth in value of the categories at constant 2005 dollars, averaged over the given periods.

more than 100 per cent of real GDP growth, offsetting negative growth in the other
two sectors.

*The international competitiveness of African manufacturers is negatively impacted
by high indirect costs related to infrastructure services.*

Inadequate infrastructure services remain a major obstacle to achieving full
economic growth potential in Africa. Addressing Africa's infrastructure will require a
substantial programme of investment, estimated at $93 billion per year (Foster and
Briceño Garmendia, eds., 2010)

Improved infrastructure and provision of services has the potential to contribute
to growth in the manufacturing sector in Africa, a sector where the competitiveness
of African firms is weak. The cost structure of firms and particularly the difference
between the direct and indirect costs of production have a bearing on the weak
competitiveness of African manufacturing. One study shows that the overall level
of profitability of African firms, which is much lower than elsewhere, results from
high indirect costs (Eifert et al., 2008). Firms in developing regions with a stronger

Figure 1. Sectoral shares of real gross domestic product by percentage and value, 2000–2012

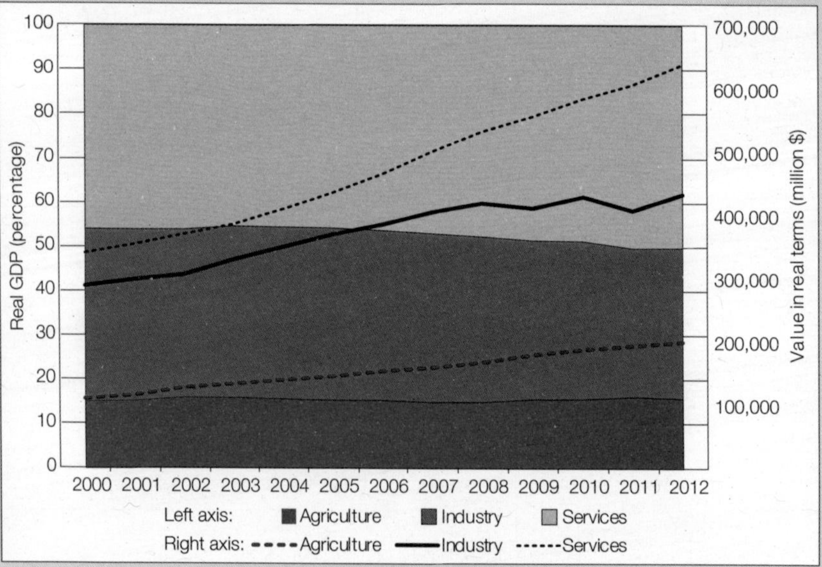

Source: UNCTAD secretariat calculations, based on data from UNCTADStat.

performance have indirect costs amounting to less than 15 per cent of total costs, whereas indirect costs in poor African countries account for 20 to 30 per cent of total costs, often exceeding labour costs. It may be seen that a considerable share of indirect costs in African firms comprises costs related to infrastructure and public services such as energy, transport, communications, water and security, which constitute significant barriers to the international competitiveness of African manufacturers.

The services sector accounted for 32.4 per cent of total employment during the period 2009–2012.

The services sector accounted for 32.4 per cent of total employment in Africa during the period 2009–2012 (International Labour Organization, 2014). As shown in figure 2, among the eight services exports-dependent economies for which employment data are available, only Cabo Verde, Liberia and Mauritius sourced more than 40 per cent of their formal employment from the services sector. Services-oriented countries do not necessarily source a large share of their formal employment from the services sector. In fact, during the period 2009–2012, the correlation coefficient between the share of services in total employment and in output was a weak 0.08. In some countries (for example Ethiopia, Mozambique, Rwanda and Zambia) where services contributed more than 40 per cent to output over the period 2009–2012, the services sector accounted for less than 20 per cent of total employment. This may be due to the nature of the services sector in these economies, the labour intensity of the services sector (for example, in tourism-dependent economies such as Mauritius and Seychelles, the services sector is highly labour intensive) and the fact that in these economies, the services sector coexists with a labour-intensive and low value added agricultural sector.

In order for the services sector in Africa to increase its contribution to employment and output, the issue of informality in the services sector will need to be addressed. The informal sector ranges from 50 to 80 per cent of GDP and 60 to 80 per cent of total employment and accounts for 90 per cent of new jobs (Benjamin and Mbaye, 2014). Some of the fastest growing sectors of West African economies (wholesale trade and retail trade, restaurants and transportation) are dominated by informal firms. African services are predominantly informal and small in scale. Addressing the issue of how to bring informal services firms into the formal sector is crucial for raising productivity and the contribution of the services sector to growth and employment.

Figure 2. Share of services in total employment by country, 2009–2012

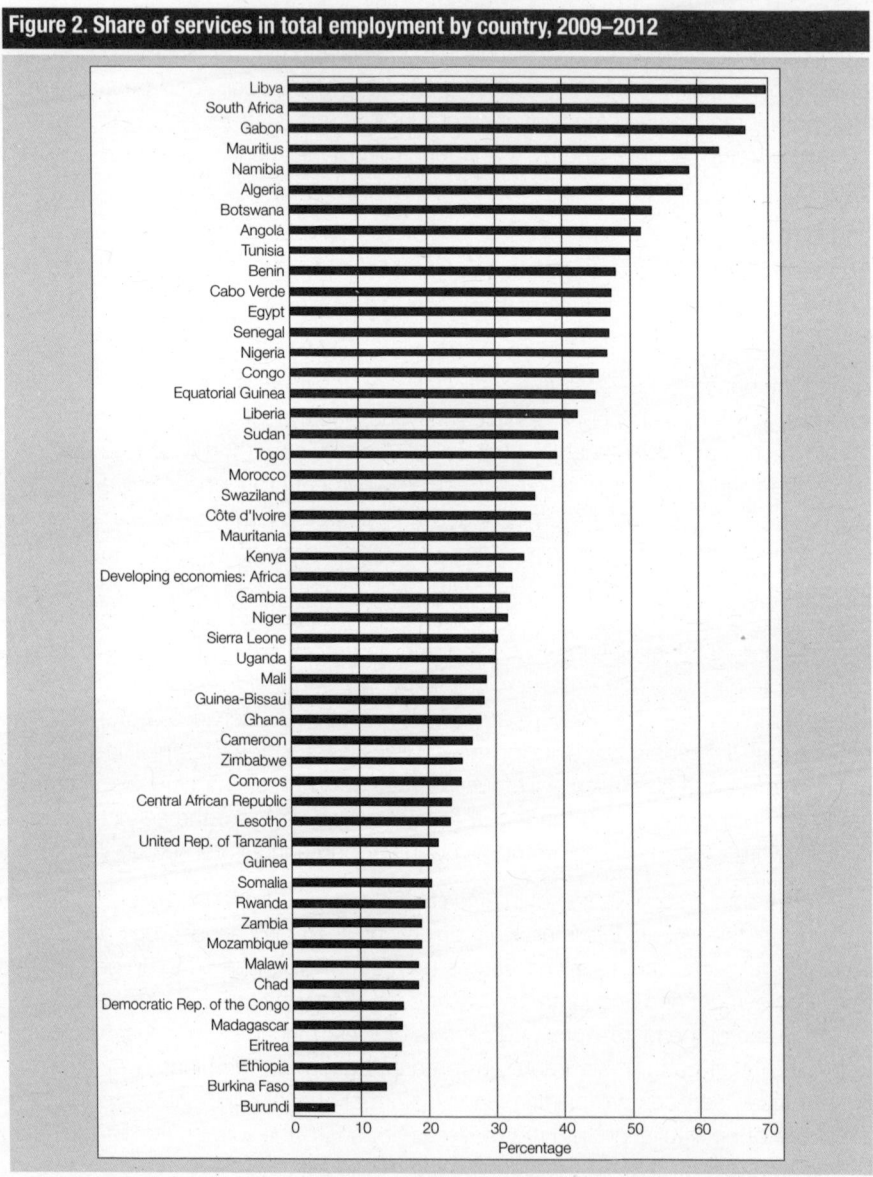

Source: International Labour Organization, 2014.
Data are not available for Djibouti, Sao Tome and Principe and Seychelles.

Relative to other regions, Africa captures only a small share of global services trade in value added terms.

There is significant potential for African countries to position themselves as services suppliers in national, regional and global value chains for goods production and in services value chains. Services are also enablers of many production and sales processes. There are important input–output linkages between manufacturing and services. With regard to South Africa, one study estimates that 25.3 per cent of the intermediate inputs into manufacturing come from services (of which the bulk comes from trade and finance) and 24.7 per cent of the intermediate inputs into services come from manufacturing (Tregenna, 2007). If imported intermediates are excluded, 31.4 per cent of all domestically produced intermediates into manufacturing are purchased from the services sector and 18.6 per cent of all domestically sourced intermediate inputs into services come from manufacturing. While African countries should aim to develop their manufacturing sectors, increasing the competitiveness of their domestic services sectors should also be a concurrent objective (UNCTAD and United Nations Industrial Development Organization, 2011). There is significant scope for African countries to position themselves as reliable and competitive services suppliers in manufacturing value chains, whether at national, regional or global levels. Global value chains can offer significant new opportunities for structural transformation in Africa. About 60 per cent of global trade consists of trade in intermediate goods and services that are incorporated at various stages in the production process of goods and services for final consumption (UNCTAD, 2013a).

To date, Africa has captured only a small share of global trade in terms of value added, although its total level of global value chain integration is high compared to other regions. However, much of this concerns the forward integration of Africa's commodity exports as inputs in foreign manufacturing, which creates little additional value added in Africa (African Development Bank et al., 2014). Upgrading over time within these value chains through process, product or functional upgrading must be a long-term policy goal for Africa in order to maximize potential economic gains from participation (UNCTAD and United Nations Industrial Development Organization, 2011, and UNCTAD, 2013a).

The successful insertion of the African services sector into global production and services value chains will depend on the ability of African countries to: build global competitiveness in the services sector; understand the determinants of competitiveness and the constraints faced by the private sector engaged in the delivery of services; and hold public–private dialogues on services issues and elaborate a clear services sector policy strategy that sets long-term development objectives for the sector.

Africa is a marginal player in global services exports and imports. Only 11 African countries have consistently been net services exporters since 2005.

In 2012, exports of services were $4.4 trillion globally and $1.3 trillion for developing countries (measured in current prices and at current exchange rates). The distribution of services exports worldwide in 2012 was as follows: 19.9 per cent in transport, 24.7 per cent in travel; and 55.4 per cent in other services, of which the largest portion was other business services.

Total imports of services in Africa amounted to an estimated $173 billion in 2012, while exports of services totalled an estimated $98 billion (UNCTADStat, February 2015). In 2012, Africa accounted for only 2.2 per cent of the world's total exports of services compared to 3.6 per cent for developing America and 24.3 per cent for developing Asia. Africa accounted for 4.0 per cent of total world services imports, compared to 5.2 per cent for developing America and 27.9 per cent for developing Asia.

Figure 3 depicts the steep rise in imports of services in Africa around 2005 and a growing divergence thereafter between services exports and imports. Services exports, in nominal terms, grew on average 9 per cent per annum between 2005 and 2009, while services imports grew at a rate of 17 per cent. In 2011 and 2012, services exports grew at around 4 per cent per annum while services imports grew at a rate of 12 per cent in 2011. Such explosive growth may reflect an ongoing liberalization process in the services sector, due to a rising demand for certain types of services associated with economic development, such as construction booms (for instance in Angola and Ethiopia) and an uncompetitive and underdeveloped formal domestic services sector. Africa's balance of trade in services as a share of GDP was -3.63 per cent in 2012 compared to 1.08 per cent for developing economies in general.

At the country level, Egypt and South Africa are Africa's two main global exporters, accounting for 0.49 per cent and 0.34 per cent of world services exports. Angola, Nigeria and South Africa are the main African global importers, accounting for more than 0.40 per cent of total world services imports.

Only the following 11 African countries have consistently been net services exporters since 2005: Cabo Verde; Djibouti; Egypt; Eritrea; Kenya; Mauritius;

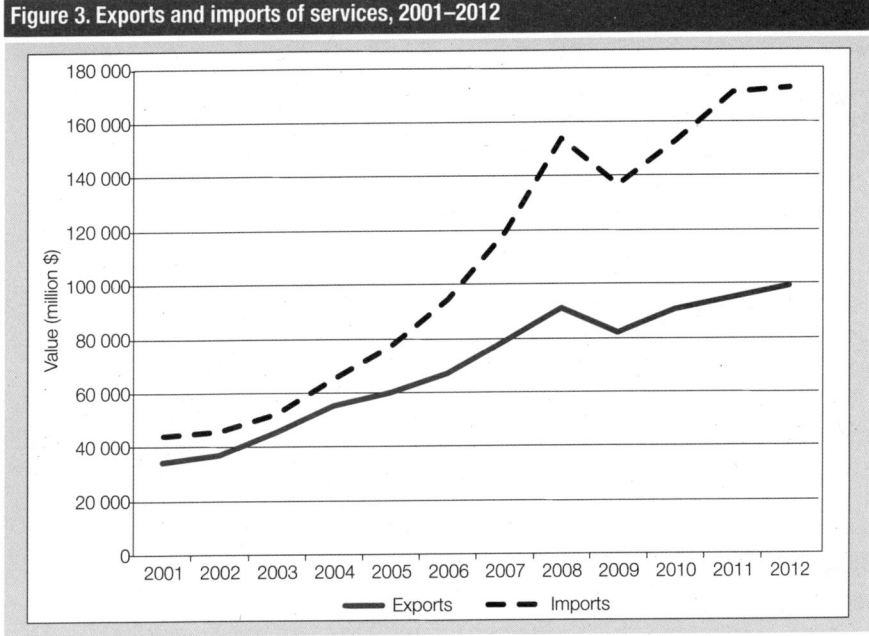

Figure 3. Exports and imports of services, 2001–2012

Source: UNCTAD secretariat calculations, based on data from UNCTADStat (accessed 1 February 2015).

Morocco; Namibia; Seychelles; Tunisia; and the United Republic of Tanzania. With the exception of Djibouti and Kenya, these countries are mainly dependent on exports of travel services (see table 5). Cabo Verde and Seychelles are among the world's 10 most tourism-intensive countries, measured as the share of tourism in GDP.

Based on averages for the period 2009–2012, the largest net services importers in Africa as a share of GDP were Liberia (-64.5 per cent), the Congo (-32.2 per cent), Angola (-21.7 per cent), Chad (-19.6 per cent) and Equatorial Guinea (-18.9 per cent). More than 60 per cent of the services imports of Chad — a landlocked country – originated in the transport sector. Over 70 per cent of the services imports of Angola, the Congo, Equatorial Guinea and Liberia originated in the other services category, that is, other than transportation and travel services. The other services category is divided into the following nine subsectors: financial; construction; communications; insurance; computers and information; Government; royalties; personal, cultural and recreational; and other business (see table 7). About 92.2

Table 5. Services exports and imports by country, averaged for 2009–2012 (Percentage shares)

Exports specialization	Exports			Imports		
	Travel	Transport	Other services	Travel	Transport	Other services
Food and agriculture						
Côte d'Ivoire	23.8	19.4	56.8	12.9	56.7	30.5
Guinea-Bissau	32.3	0.9	66.8	29.4	37.6	33.0
Malawi	37.5	27.5	35.0	35.0	13.5	51.5
Somalia	..	..	..	0.0	42.3	57.7
Fuels						
Algeria	6.4	21.0	72.6	4.3	28.1	67.5
Angola	87.1	4.1	8.8	0.7	18.4	80.9
Chad	37.5	1.6	60.8	12.0	65.7	22.3
Congo	17.0	3.8	79.2	4.7	15.0	80.3
Equatorial Guinea	45.1	1.1	53.8	4.8	20.4	74.8
Gabon	6.3	18.1	75.6	26.3	30.7	42.9
Libya	6.9	69.7	23.4	38.3	34.1	27.6
Nigeria	21.8	54.6	23.6	26.4	36.4	37.2
South Sudan	..	..	..	..	..	..
Sudan	52.1	1.9	46.0	43.1	45.9	11.1
Manufactured goods						
Lesotho	60.8	1.3	37.9	57.9	14.1	27.9
Tunisia	44.6	26.9	28.5	16.7	49.1	34.3
Mixed exporters						
Benin	45.3	22.1	32.6	9.9	61.2	28.9
Burkina Faso	26.3	16.0	57.7	8.1	45.9	46.0
Burundi	2.3	1.8	96.0	18.3	58.2	23.4
Cameroon	19.7	35.8	44.5	20.9	38.5	40.6
Central African Republic	20.6	3.4	76.0	32.8	52.1	15.1
Egypt	48.4	37.0	14.6	16.3	44.4	39.4
Eritrea	63.0	27.7	9.3	48.1	28.1	23.8
Ghana	37.6	25.3	37.1	16.5	40.4	43.1
Kenya	21.8	41.9	36.3	9.9	49.0	41.1
Morocco	52.3	18.5	29.2	15.9	37.4	46.8
Mozambique	29.5	27.8	42.7	13.0	28.6	58.4
Namibia	55.9	15.9	28.1	23.4	37.7	38.9
Niger	73.7	5.7	20.6	6.7	71.1	22.2
Senegal	40.6	7.0	52.4	12.6	51.9	35.5
Sierra Leone	30.2	23.3	46.5	5.2	52.0	42.8

Table 5 (continued)

Exports specialization	Exports			Imports		
	Travel	Transport	Other services	Travel	Transport	Other services
South Africa	64.6	11.5	23.8	27.0	41.4	31.6
Swaziland	14.8	13.5	71.7	9.6	14.3	76.1
Togo	21.2	38.3	40.5	11.8	62.2	26.0
Uganda	58.4	5.9	35.7	17.0	55.7	27.3
United Republic of Tanzania	60.5	21.9	17.6	42.5	40.4	17.1
Zimbabwe	44.6	38.8	16.6	4.6	79.9	15.5
Ores and metals						
Botswana	17.1	10.0	72.9	11.1	15.9	73.0
Democratic Rep. of the Congo	2.8	19.9	77.3	6.9	47.7	45.4
Guinea	2.7	9.0	88.4	3.6	43.6	52.9
Mali	50.2	2.7	47.2	10.9	61.2	27.9
Mauritania	59.4	1.9	38.7	27.8	31.8	40.4
Zambia	38.2	48.4	13.4	6.9	54.0	39.1
Services						
Cabo Verde	62.1	27.8	10.1	42.1	36.4	21.5
Comoros	55.2	5.2	39.6	19.7	62.3	18.1
Djibouti	5.6	34.6	59.8	9.0	60.3	30.7
Gambia	58.0	28.4	13.6	12.8	55.5	31.7
Ethiopia	22.3	55.7	22.0	5.5	65.5	29.0
Liberia	32.4	15.8	51.8	4.5	7.9	87.6
Madagascar	35.3	30.7	34.0	9.7	40.2	50.1
Mauritius	46.7	13.2	40.1	18.3	27.1	54.5
Rwanda	58.2	12.0	29.9	14.0	61.3	24.7
Sao Tome and Principe	83.7	1.3	15.0	1.0	80.2	18.8
Seychelles	64.2	28.2	7.5	15.2	50.4	34.3
Developing economies: Africa	*45.3*	*25.6*	*29.1*	*16.2*	*36.7*	*47.1*

Source: UNCTAD secretariat calculations, based on data from UNCTADStat.

per cent of other services imports in Liberia were accounted for by government services, while in Angola, the Congo and Equatorial Guinea, about 48 per cent were accounted for by other business services. Some of these countries are undergoing significant post-conflict reconstruction, and the provision of private sector services has broken down and has yet to be fully restored.

With regard to services, the existence of low levels of exports and high levels of imports must be interpreted with caution and should not necessarily be associated with poor economic performance. A high level of services imports could reflect growing demand for services as an input in quickly growing productive sectors, while a low level of services exports may suggest that more domestic services are being used to relieve supply bottlenecks in the domestic economy.

Figure 4 shows the distribution of imports and exports of services in Africa in 2013. The five major imports subsectors in 2013 were transport, travel, construction, government services and other business services. Together, these five subsectors accounted for about 72 per cent of total services imports in Africa. The five major exports subsectors were travel, transport, government services, other business services and communications, which totalled 87 per cent.

This chapter highlights, through a series of stylized facts, the actual contribution of the services sector to African economies in terms of output, employment and exports. The services sector has the potential to contribute to structural transformation, economic growth and development in Africa if concerted efforts are made to tackle sectoral informality, generate more formal jobs and implement development strategies. African countries should aim to exploit the potential complementarities and linkages between the services sector and other productive sectors of the economy. Policies should also facilitate the insertion of African services suppliers into global value chains and regional value chains in both goods and services.

Figure 4.   Distribution of exports and imports of services, 2013 (Percentage shares)

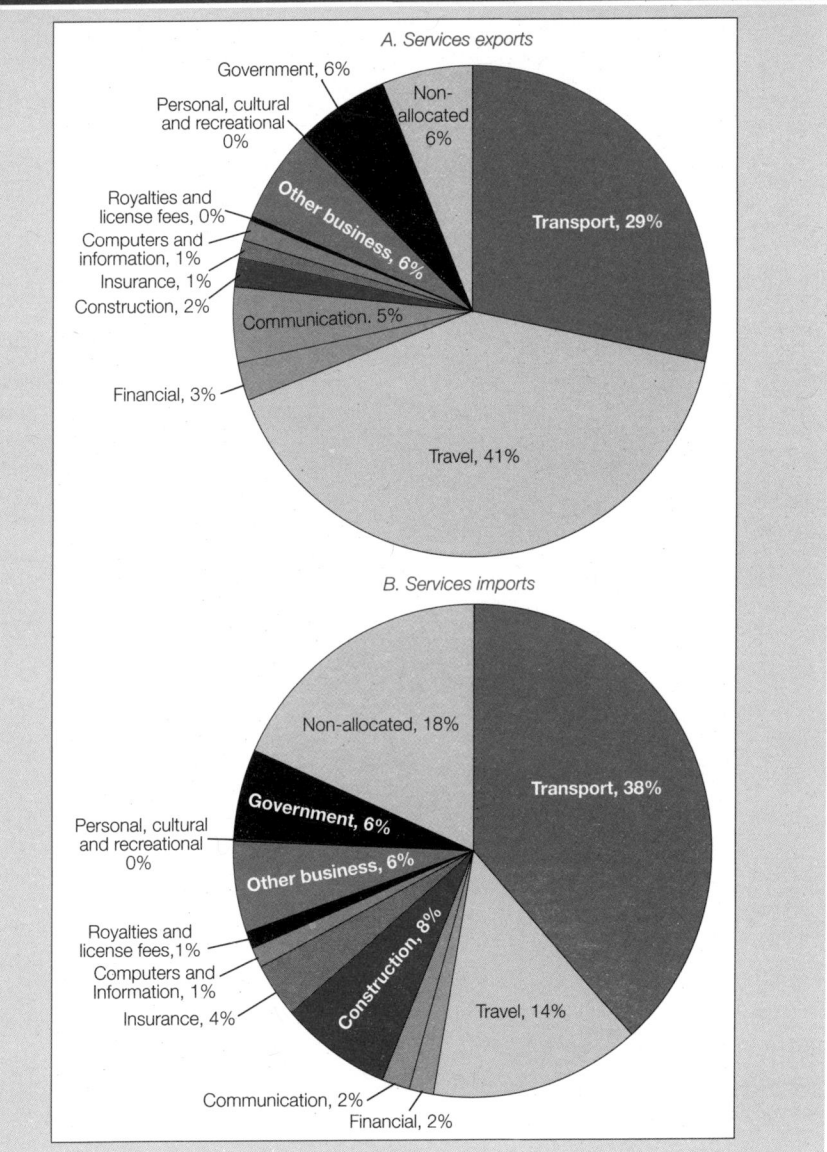

A. Services exports

Government, 6%
Personal, cultural and recreational 0%
Non-allocated 6%
Royalties and license fees, 0%
Computers and information, 1%
Insurance, 1%
Construction, 2%
Financial, 3%
Other business, 6%
Communication. 5%
Transport, 29%
Travel, 41%

B. Services imports

Non-allocated, 18%
Personal, cultural and recreational 0%
Government, 6%
Other business, 6%
Royalties and license fees, 1%
Computers and Information, 1%
Insurance, 4%
Construction, 8%
Communication, 2%
Financial, 2%
Transport, 38%
Travel, 14%

Source: UNCTAD secretariat calculations, based on data from UNCTADStat.

Table 6. Other services exports by country, averaged for 2009–2012 (Percentage shares)

Exports specialization	Finan-cial	Constru-ction	Communi-cation	Insurance	Compu-ters and informa-tion	Govern-ment	Royalties	Personal, cultural and recre-ational	Other business
Food and agriculture									
Côte d'Ivoire	10.1	0.9	16.1	6.4	0.9	26.5	0.0	0.0	39.2
Guinea-Bissau	14.6	1.1	61.5	1.1	2.4	5.3	2.8	0.4	10.8
Malawi	14.0	2.4	34.6	4.7	1.4	18.3	0.0	2.4	22.2
Somalia	..	..	..	..	..	..	..	..	..
Fuels									
Algeria	8.5	6.3	6.4	3.0	0.7	5.2	0.1	0.2	69.7
Angola	1.5	8.2	57.2	0.5	1.2	0.0	1.4	24.6	5.3
Chad	2.6	1.0	0.9	0.9	2.1	80.4	2.4	0.3	9.3
Congo	12.6	4.6	4.4	4.3	9.9	6.6	11.5	1.5	44.5
Equatorial Guinea	2.3	0.9	0.8	0.8	1.8	82.6	2.1	0.3	8.3
Gabon	7.1	2.6	2.5	26.2	5.5	23.5	6.5	0.8	25.2
Libya	0.0	0.0	37.8	..	..	..	..	..	..
Nigeria	2.0	0.0	7.8	0.2	0.0	84.6	0.0	0.0	5.3
South Sudan	..	..	..	..	..	..	..	..	..
Sudan	7.8	8.9	14.0	0.9	0.3	55.9	1.0	0.5	10.8
Manufactured goods									
Lesotho	2.9	0.0	20.4	6.0	2.3	27.5	0.0	0.0	41.0
Tunisia	4.4	26.9	20.0	4.1	2.7	20.6	1.7	0.6	19.0
Mixed exporters									
Benin	8.8	3.7	25.4	2.8	0.2	19.2	0.0	0.2	39.6
Burkina Faso	13.0	21.0	41.2	1.2	1.7	12.9	0.2	0.5	8.3
Burundi	0.5	2.6	0.3	1.9	0.6	91.4	0.2	0.0	2.6
Cameroon	2.1	0.5	10.9	7.5	0.2	12.2	0.0	7.3	59.3
Central African Republic	3.4	1.2	1.2	1.2	2.6	75.1	3.1	0.4	11.9
Egypt	5.2	18.9	27.1	3.6	5.7	7.6	2.6	3.5	25.8
Eritrea	13.5	5.0	4.7	4.6	10.6	0.0	12.4	1.6	47.7
Ghana	0.0	0.0	6.6	3.2	0.0	22.2	0.0	0.0	68.0
Kenya	7.9	0.0	28.8	2.5	0.0	57.5	2.9	0.4	0.0
Morocco	1.1	1.3	18.7	3.9	8.8	11.0	0.1	1.2	54.0
Mozambique	1.3	7.2	11.4	1.1	1.9	23.3	0.2	0.9	52.7

Table 6 (continued)

Exports specialization	Finan-cial	Constru-ction	Communi-cation	Insurance	Compu-ters and informa-tion	Govern-ment	Royalties	Personal, cultural and recre-ational	Other business
Namibia	1.3	0.0	6.1	1.6	0.4	8.1	0.0	0.0	82.5
Niger	14.1	1.1	22.6	4.1	2.1	14.7	2.3	0.3	38.7
Senegal	1.0	11.2	30.6	2.3	4.7	21.7	0.3	0.1	28.2
Sierra Leone	1.6	1.7	69.3	1.3	3.6	1.1	4.1	0.5	16.5
South Africa	25.0	1.8	6.3	8.3	8.6	11.9	1.8	2.0	34.3
Swaziland	6.0	18.4	9.9	6.2	0.3	5.6	3.0	1.2	49.3
Togo	8.6	3.2	41.9	1.8	0.0	24.1	5.3	0.5	25.4
Uganda	4.1	17.1	4.7	3.3	8.5	39.1	1.4	0.4	21.3
United Republic of Tanzania	1.6	6.1	10.6	7.5	1.2	12.0	0.0	0.7	60.3
Zimbabwe	0.0	0.0	3.1	13.3	3.8	45.1	2.1	1.2	31.4
Ores and metals									
Botswana	0.6	2.8	7.2	9.2	1.2	19.8	0.1	0.0	59.1
Democratic Rep. of the Congo	13.6	1.5	19.7	1.3	0.0	40.5	0.0	1.6	21.9
Guinea	0.0	18.0	41.2	13.8	0.2	6.1	0.0	5.9	14.7
Mali	2.6	2.1	72.7	2.5	0.0	16.1	0.5	0.4	3.2
Mauritania	3.7	1.4	1.3	1.3	2.9	72.6	3.4	0.4	13.0
Zambia	0.0	0.0	54.4	16.7	0.0	0.0	0.0	· 19.7	9.2
Services									
Cabo Verde	4.0	0.4	47.7	11.1	0.2	32.4	0.0	0.2	4.1
Comoros	0.0	0.0	63.8	0.5	0.0	35.7	0.0	0.0	0.0
Djibouti	0.6	0.2	4.2	0.2	0.5	91.6	0.5	0.1	2.1
Gambia	0.0	21.6	58.6	18.7	1.1	0.0	0.0	0.0	0.0
Ethiopia	1.0	4.9	24.9	0.4	0.1	44.5	0.1	0.0	24.2
Liberia	0.3	0.1	0.1	0.1	0.2	97.9	0.3	0.0	1.0
Madagascar	3.8	5.5	6.9	2.6	4.0	12.1	7.7	0.3	57.1
Mauritius	8.9	2.6	7.1	3.4	3.9	3.0	0.1	2.1	69.1
Rwanda	0.6	1.4	22.2	0.8	0.0	66.7	5.2	0.0	3.2
Sao Tome and Principe	19.7	0.6	53.8	0.5	1.2	17.2	1.4	0.2	5.4
Seychelles	10.2	3.7	24.7	3.0	8.0	1.7	11.4	1.2	36.1

Source: UNCTAD secretariat calculations, based on data from UNCTADStat.
Note: Figures relate to the share of each category in other services.

Table 7.   Other services imports by country, averaged for 2009–2012 (Percentage shares)

Exports specialization	Financial	Constru-ction	Comuni-cation	Insu-rance	Comput-ers and informa-tion	Govern-ment	Royalties	Personal, cultural and recre-ational	Other business
Food and agriculture									
Côte d'Ivoire	15.8	2.7	9.1	10.7	1.8	24.9	2.2	0.1	32.6
Guinea-Bissau	0.5	0.2	11.5	11.0	5.3	6.9	0.0	17.0	47.7
Malawi	3.7	2.5	6.9	18.6	1.0	30.2	0.5	10.0	26.5
Somalia	6.9	4.8	4.9	9.5	6.7	0.0	15.9	2.2	49.1
Fuels									
Algeria	0.7	30.4	1.1	2.5	0.8	5.7	1.1	0.3	57.5
Angola	2.5	34.2	2.7	1.6	0.3	9.0	0.0	1.0	48.7
Chad	6.4	4.4	4.5	8.9	6.2	7.1	14.7	2.1	45.6
Congo	6.9	4.8	4.9	9.5	6.7	0.2	15.8	2.2	49.0
Equatorial Guinea	6.8	4.7	4.8	9.3	6.6	2.2	15.5	2.2	48.0
Gabon	6.6	4.6	4.7	9.1	6.4	4.8	15.1	2.1	46.7
Libya	0.0	2.9	2.8	..	..	..	..	..	0.0
Nigeria	2.4	1.2	4.0	7.0	2.0	22.3	2.8	0.6	57.7
South Sudan	..	..	..	..	..	..	..	..	..
Sudan	6.2	2.0	6.9	19.8	2.9	50.3	2.0	2.0	7.9
Manufactured goods									
Lesotho	1.2	4.2	4.8	13.3	1.5	25.7	3.2	2.0	44.1
Tunisia	5.9	30.9	5.4	19.2	2.7	16.5	1.2	0.8	17.5
Mixed exporters									
Benin	3.4	8.6	22.1	15.3	4.7	6.1	1.7	0.0	38.1
Burkina Faso	6.3	11.6	10.9	27.0	4.9	5.4	0.1	0.0	33.9
Burundi	3.2	3.3	3.2	6.5	4.4	41.8	4.5	0.6	32.5
Cameroon	3.7	4.9	5.1	16.5	0.5	6.1	1.3	0.4	61.4
Central African Rep.	6.8	4.7	4.8	9.3	6.6	2.2	15.5	2.2	48.0
Egypt	0.8	5.3	6.5	25.4	2.1	20.4	4.7	1.0	33.9
Eritrea	6.9	4.8	4.9	9.5	6.7	0.0	15.9	2.2	49.1
Ghana	4.1	2.9	2.9	9.4	4.0	36.3	9.5	1.3	29.5
Kenya	8.3	3.4	13.0	13.2	0.2	21.5	2.5	0.8	37.0
Morocco	1.7	0.1	2.4	5.3	1.7	46.5	1.2	0.7	40.3
Mozambique	1.6	37.8	4.2	1.5	1.7	5.2	0.5	0.3	47.1
Namibia	1.6	17.7	0.1	10.4	11.9	3.0	2.5	2.3	50.6
Niger	5.9	19.6	26.1	8.9	7.1	0.0	4.4	0.6	27.5
Senegal	3.8	10.7	17.5	27.1	4.7	9.5	1.7	0.0	25.0
Sierra Leone	0.2	5.5	9.5	11.4	1.2	9.3	0.6	2.7	59.7

Table 7 (continued)

Exports specialization	Financial	Constru-ction	Comuni-cation	Insurance	Comput-ers and informa-tion	Govern-ment	Royalties	Personal, cultural and recre-ational	Other business
South Africa	2.4	0.1	6.3	9.9	3.4	8.0	34.7	0.2	34.9
Swaziland	2.6	1.7	3.2	3.4	8.4	3.7	13.5	0.1	63.3
Togo	2.3	9.8	16.2	37.6	8.7	6.3	5.8	0.6	25.4
Uganda	1.3	15.7	4.0	14.2	6.8	4.5	1.1	2.2	50.4
United Rep. of Tanzania	1.1	7.1	6.9	20.3	3.2	13.4	3.4	0.1	44.4
Zimbabwe	0.0	0.0	6.4	4.5	6.7	3.0	11.6	2.7	65.1
Ores and metals									
Botswana	1.5	3.6	7.2	11.5	2.1	25.8	2.1	2.8	43.3
Dem. Rep. of the Congo	5.3	3.2	1.1	28.9	3.3	20.2	4.1	1.2	32.6
Guinea	6.8	6.1	4.9	13.7	0.8	17.4	0.3	1.0	48.9
Mali	1.7	20.1	25.5	13.4	4.0	4.6	0.4	0.4	29.9
Mauritania	4.3	3.0	3.1	6.0	4.2	37.4	9.9	1.4	30.7
Zambia	1.4	32.1	3.0	29.2	1.3	10.4	0.1	1.2	21.3
Services									
Cabo Verde	3.7	2.3	10.1	26.4	10.8	14.8	3.3	1.2	27.4
Comoros	0.0	0.0	7.9	65.0	3.0	3.7	0.0	2.5	17.9
Djibouti	2.6	1.8	1.9	27.0	2.6	38.5	6.0	0.8	18.7
Gambia	2.8	4.7	18.3	43.7	3.1	0.0	6.4	0.9	20.1
Ethiopia	0.3	44.4	9.7	13.6	0.5	2.3	0.3	0.9	28.0
Liberia	0.5	0.3	1.3	0.2	0.5	92.2	1.1	0.5	3.4
Madagascar	1.1	1.5	7.0	1.0	1.6	20.1	4.2	0.1	63.5
Mauritius	9.3	2.0	5.0	5.6	1.2	3.2	1.0	5.6	67.2
Rwanda	0.8	2.2	19.4	3.4	0.2	70.3	0.4	0.1	3.2
Sao Tome and Principe	4.0	0.5	4.7	29.7	0.7	53.8	1.6	0.2	4.9
Seychelles	7.7	8.1	1.2	10.3	7.3	6.3	1.6	2.5	55.0

Source: UNCTAD secretariat calculations, based on data from UNCTADStat.
Note: Figures relate to the share of each category in other services.

Box 1. Conceptualizing and defining services in Africa

Definitional issues

Services may be defined as changes in the condition of an economic agent (including a person) or in the condition of a good or asset (wealth) belonging to an economic agent, as a result of some activity of a second economic agent, carried out with the prior agreement of the first agent.

The System of National Accounts of the United Nations distinguishes the following three categories of services:

- *Change-effecting services:* Services that may lead to changes in the physical condition of an agent or good (e.g. car or home repairs, medical procedures and haircuts), or the mental condition of an agent (e.g. education and legal services). The change in condition brought about by such services may be temporary or permanent.

- *Margin services:* Changes in condition that facilitate the exchange of other goods or assets or services between the user of such services and another party (who may or may not be the producer of the service). Such services include wholesale and retail distribution activities and changes in condition related to the physical location of an agent or its goods (transportation) or an agent's current wealth or risks facing future wealth (financial services) or the social condition of an agent by enabling interaction (connection) with other agents (communications).

- *Knowledge-capturing products:* Hybrid products, with characteristics of both goods and services (e.g. newspapers, electronic media and digital information). Such products have a physical existence; ownership rights can terefore be established and transferability is possible. The knowledge they store may be accessed more than once and production and consumption are not necessarily simultaneous. However, they are like services in that their content (the information and knowledge they contain) changes the mental condition of the user, either temporarily or permanently.

The first characteristic of services is that they are produced and consumed (or used) simultaneously. Production is the activity bringing about the relevant change in condition and use is the change in condition itself. For many services, particularly if the change in condition is a physical change to a person or a good, a second characteristic follows as a corollary of the first: the producer and user must be in the same location. The third characteristic of services is that they are intangible and cannot be stored, that is, because they are changes in condition, they cannot be produced in advance of their use. They are only produced once demand for them exists. Finally, services are unlike goods in that they are not transferable separately from their production. Agents cannot purchase services separately from their use in order to establish ownership rights over the services and transfer them to third parties.

The need for simultaneous production and consumption when services are traded internationally focuses attention on another set of characteristics of services, the mode of supply (i.e. the process through which the producer and user come into contact). Under some circumstances, cross-border trade (referred to as mode 1 in GATS) is possible, where the producer and user are located in different countries and export and import, respectively. For some services (e.g. tourism and surgical procedures), users from importing countries must move temporarily to the exporting country (consumption abroad, mode 2). A services producer may also move from an exporting country in order to provide services to users in an importing country, either by locating a permanent operation in the country via a capital investment (commercial presence, mode 3) or by temporarily migrating labour to provide the services (presence of natural persons, mode 4).

Box 1 (continued)

Measurement issues

Measurement of services output (value added) and international trade in services is subject to two major challenges, which follow from the definitional characteristics discussed above.

The first challenge is measuring the real output of services activities and the volume of international trade in services. Measuring real output, adjusted for inflation, requires a price index, which assumes that what is defined as a single unit of the product does not change over time in either quantity or quality. Assuming unchanged quality is an issue for both goods and services, especially in defining whether a product with features that are new compared with earlier versions should be considered a new product or a new model of an original product. However, for services, even assuming constant quantity over time is not straightforward, due to difficulties in defining a single unit of a services product, as services are heterogeneous and difficult to standardize and the nature of the product often depends in part on the user as well as the producer (e.g. in education services).

The second challenge of measurement arises from the need for many services inputs in the production of both goods and services. Input services such as financial management or factory cleaning may be provided by the producer of an output, in which case they are not measured separately as a services output. Alternatively, they may be sourced from an independent services producer, in which case they are measured separately. Output and employment in services are higher in the former scenario, even though actual economic activity may not be different.

Another issue with regard to measurement, of particular relevance to Africa, relates to informal sector activities, which overlaps (but is not identical with) what is referred to as the non-observed economy in the System of National Accounts. The informal sector in general has a greater predominance of services sector activities than manufacturing or other industrial activities, in part because the entry barriers to many services activities are low, especially in low-income market segments in developing countries. Both household and enterprise surveys are used to measure informal sector activity, often in combination, but these are imperfect instruments, especially in developing countries. Although considerable progress has been made in developing agreed definitions and approaches to measuring informal sector output, there is as yet no standardized approach, making cross-country comparison difficult (United Nations, 2009).

Measuring international trade in services can pose particular challenges over and above those faced in the measurement of services value added. Mode 1 transactions require foreign currency exchanges and as a result are, in principle, recorded and included in the current accounts of the balance of payments as non-factor services. However, the growth of e-commerce has made it much more difficult to record international trade in margin services. With regard to mode 2, services production and use occur within the territory of an importing country, with no exchange of foreign currency or customs declarations attached to individual transactions. In principle this should not make a difference to the measurement of value added and employment, yet it may be difficult to identify a transaction as involving international trade. For instance, it is difficult to distinguish the purchase of a restaurant meal or visit to a local museum by a foreign tourist from the same purchases made by a domestic resident.

International services trade via modes 3 and 4 is less complicated conceptually. Services trade via mode 3 (commercial presence or direct investment in a host country by a foreign services provider) is counted in principle as part of the host economy's national accounting system. The amount supplied by foreign providers (imported, in terms of the GATS conceptual framework) is used to develop foreign affiliate statistics data, detailed in the Manual on Statistics on

Box 1 (continued)

International Trade in Services of the United Nations Department of Economic and Social Affairs, which notes that there are currently few reliable international comparisons of foreign affiliate statistics. Only some member countries of the Organization for Economic Cooperation and Development (OECD) have developed this data and such data is not available for Africa, as it is not a priority in the allocation of already-scarce resources for statistics collection and construction.

Services trade via mode 4 involves the temporary migration of labour from an exporting to an importing country to produce services for users in the latter, for example an employee of a South African investment bank moving to Kenya to arrange financing for a new power station for a Kenyan electricity company. Payment for the individual's services would be a cross-border transaction and recorded in the current accounts of the balance of payments of the importing and exporting countries under factor services.

It may be noted that there is a considerable amount of international trade in services in the context of the informal sector and unrecorded economy in Africa, given the relative porosity of borders and the large numbers of temporary and permanent migrants throughout the continent.

Categorizing services

There are essentially two approaches to categorizing services, depending on the object of measurement. Measures of value added and other national accounts variables defined by the System of National Accounts follow the International Standard Industrial Classification of All Economic Activities, in which sectors are classified into primary, secondary and tertiary groups, based on their relationship with and distance from natural resources.* Services make up the tertiary sector, including wholesale trade and retail trade, restaurants and hotels, transportation and storage, information and communications, finance and insurance, real estate, professional, scientific and technical, government (including defence, education and health) and other services. In the International Standard Industrial Classification hierarchy, construction, followed by electricity, gas and water, are placed before wholesale trade and retail trade, and these two sets of activities may be included in either the secondary or tertiary sectors.

A sectoral classification for internationally traded services is detailed in the sixth edition of the Balance of Payments and International Investment Position Manual of the International Monetary Fund (IMF), which differs from the International Standard Industrial Classification (the Harmonized System used to classify traded goods also differs from the International Standard Industrial Classification). The main categories are as follows: manufacturing services on physical inputs owned by others; maintenance and repair services; transport, travel and construction; insurance and pensions; financial services; charges for the use of intellectual property; ICT; other business services; personal, cultural and recreational services; and government goods and services (IMF, 2009). Wholesale trade and retail trade services are included in the cost of the goods distributed by services.

The differences between the two frameworks therefore complicate the analysis of services trade growth linkages at sectoral and national levels.

* Some countries use their own variations of the International Standard Industrial Classification, such as the Statistical Classification of Economic Activities in the European Community, the General Classification of Economic Activities in Switzerland and the North American Industry Classification System in the United States.

CHAPTER 2

MAKING REGULATION WORK FOR SERVICES IN AFRICA

A. INTRODUCTION

The services sector plays an important role in Africa's economic and social development. However, Africa has not been able to fully capitalize on the sector, and services provision is suboptimal and entails high costs. Many of the market failures and inefficiencies afflicting the sector may be addressed through regulation.

This chapter examines the economic development potential of the regulation of the infrastructure services sector (whether public or privately owned) and how regulation may contribute to bridging Africa's infrastructure gap in order to promote economic development. In addition, this chapter discusses how domestic regulatory and institutional frameworks might improve the provision of infrastructural services, and the analysis of regulatory provision focuses specifically on the means of enhancing the contribution of regulated infrastructure services to growth and development in Africa.

B. WHAT ARE INFRASTRUCTURE SERVICES AND WHY IS THEIR REGULATION IMPORTANT?

A critical constraint to realizing economic growth potential in Africa is the state of infrastructure services (transport, telecommunications, water, energy and sanitation). Infrastructure services critical to social development, health and economic growth are provided via physical networks (e.g. electricity wires, gas pipelines and sewage pipe systems) and mainly through local or national monopoly facilities. These services are highly capital intensive, are mainly comprised of sunk assets (i.e. immovable equipment with little second-hand value) and are characterized by considerable economies of scale and scope.

Since the 1980s, privatized infrastructure services have grown and demand for effective utility regulation has increased largely because of the poor financial performance of many (State-owned) utilities, inappropriate pricing policies (often due to political pressures) and unsustainable subsidization of services for certain categories of customers. In addition, most African countries face stringent limitations on public sector finance for new capacity in transport, telecommunications, water and energy infrastructure, and wish to accelerate services provision to foster economic growth (World Economic Forum et al., 2009). As infrastructure services industries are typically dependent on monopolistic networks (whether public or privately owned or local and/or national), economic regulation needs to address concerns about competition (asymmetries of information and abuse of dominance) and consumer interests (universal access, affordability and quality). With the increasing integration of infrastructure systems across Africa through pan-territorial initiatives (e.g. Programme for Infrastructure Development in Africa) and common electricity markets, potentially significant benefits from economies of scale and shared resources require effective regional regulation.[3]

Infrastructure services regulation is also critical as a guarantor of access, affordability and quality control, which are interconnected. For example, if high technical, health, safety or environmental standards are not achieved, the poorest segments of society cannot afford formal infrastructure services and consequently rely on low quality and unsafe informal and unregulated suppliers. The type of regulation matters; simply regulating inputs or processes rather than outputs or outcomes may reduce a utility or firm's incentive to improve quality, access and efficiency. If a country decides to open up the sector, the sequencing of privatization and development of regulatory institutions are also important, as establishing an institutional framework conducive to promoting competition and governing access, affordability and quality control before privatizing infrastructure services is correlated with improved investment and wider services provision (Zhang et al., 2004, and UNCTAD, 2012).

Since the 1980s, it has become both technologically and commercially possible to separate infrastructure networks (e.g. electricity transmission lines and railways) from services provision and, as a consequence, to introduce competition in some segments of the market. This has fundamentally changed the nature of regulation, but has not lessened the need for it, particularly where infrastructure services are unbundled (or separated) from traditional monopoly utilities.

In recent years, there has been growing recognition that significant welfare gains may be realized through deep forms of regional integration that entail the harmonization of legal, regulatory and institutional frameworks. Reforms that reduce cross-border transaction costs and improve the performance of infrastructure services are arguably as important for the creation of an open and unified regional economic space as trade policy reforms (Kessides et al., 2009).

The preferred institutional organization of regulation is generally a body appointed or authorized by the Government, but independent of it, and thus less subject to political or electoral pressures (see box 2).[4] With regard to professional services (credibility products) the market is often self-regulated by the collective action of providers, though the State may provide them legal authority to do so. Establishing the independent economic regulation of network utilities and infrastructure services (transport, telecommunications, water and energy, including petroleum, piped gas and electricity) has emerged as a key economic policy issue in the past 30 years, with the rise of public utility privatization.

Regulation in infrastructure involves (at least) the following four elements: market access and barriers to entry; operational regulation and pricing; competition; and investment requirements for services providers. The latter element is significant in Africa, where networks are often quite limited in range and poorly maintained, but private providers may be reluctant to expand and upgrade.

National Governments define policy for public services and regulate many private services markets. This applies in particular to infrastructure services (transport, telecommunications, water and energy), financial services, education, health care and professional services (medical, legal, engineering, accounting and auditing), that is, services that display some public good characteristics and/or that are credibility products whose quality may be difficult to assess even after consumption.

The need for regulation of such essential economic infrastructure and utility services is critical for three reasons. First, for achieving post-2015 sustainable development goals related to social welfare, water and sanitation and health-related indicators, greater emphasis is placed on regulation that protects consumers, attracts investors and enables Governments to achieve policy objectives (Stern and Cubbin, 2005). Second, Africa's infrastructure services, in particular road freight, are more expensive and of lower quality than in any other region of the world (African Development Bank, 2010). Inland transport costs are much higher than elsewhere. One study estimated that international transport costs faced by African countries, at 12.6 per cent of the delivered value of exports, were more than twice as high as the world average of 6.1 per cent (International Labour Organization, 2014, and UNCTAD, 2003). In addition, freight moves slowly and uncertainly and the reduction in trade resulting from poor transport performance could exceed 20 per cent (Infrastructure Consortium for Africa, 2013). Third, access to electricity is low across Africa and the amount of electricity being generated, reliably and consistently, is too low to meet rising demand (Vagliasindi and Nellis, 2009).

What are the key features of a modern regulatory framework?

There is growing consensus on the key design features of a modern regulatory framework and ancillary agency (see box 2). The main features of effective regulation of privatized utilities are coherence, independence, accountability, predictability, transparency and capacity, along with accessibility, affordability, ownership and quality control (Brown et al., 2006). Coherence implies that the laws underpinning regulation are consistent, with clear divisions of responsibility between municipal and national regulators. Predictability relates to overall decision-making stability in the regulatory framework, as confidence in the decision-making processes of a regulatory body is important for long-term investors in network industries. Capacity relates to the quality of human resources available to the authority and appropriate levels of staffing. Regulatory bodies should be strengthened, allowed to operate independently and adapted to fit the specific needs of each State.

The structure of infrastructure services industries is of critical importance, not least in defining the role of regulation. In addition, the nature of a Government's infrastructure services policy will determine how important liberalization and competition are in a given industry. A key consideration in establishing an effective regulatory framework for infrastructure services is industry characteristics (e.g. the size of the market), with a particular focus on the nature of demand and rate of technical progress, both of which have implications for market entry and competition. Typically, infrastructure services with a high or rising level of demand and a faster rate of technological progress, such as telecommunications, tend to be more attractive to new market entrants and may have lower barriers to entry, reducing the need for extensive regulation. However, this needs to be balanced against other areas where infrastructure networks require regulation to monitor equal market access and avoid the market dominance of an incumbent (whether public or privately owned), for example with regard to electricity transmission lines and railway rolling stock and tracks.

A key element of any regulatory framework for infrastructure services is tariff setting. Regulatory bodies need to develop transparent and predictable procedures for tariff setting without reducing the incentive of infrastructure services providers and operators to increase efficiency. Most regulation regimes focus on either a form of price-cap or rate-of-return regulation. In theory, price-cap regulation should encourage greater efficiency, as operators attempt to lower operational costs to make a profit but, in fact, the difference between the two approaches in developing countries is quite small (Brown et al., 2006). Conventional cost-plus pricing used to be widespread in Europe, based on the costs of utilities, plus a return to compensate for their activity. Today, only a few countries allow distribution and transmission system operators to automatically pass along costs in their tariffs.

Box 2. Typology of a regulatory and/or institutional framework for infrastructure services

The key objectives of economic regulation involve regulation of the following:

- Prices and/or rates of return on assets
- Quality of services
- Investment and/or development plans (regulatory investment plans in monopoly networks)

A regulatory authority is typically responsible for implementing and developing the regulatory framework. In countries with regulatory best practice, there is usually a clear structure to the framework, comprising primary law, licenses and/or secondary legislation and detailed codes on services obligations, technical codes and performance standards. Each code and standard assists in regulation of a particular aspect of industry conduct.

A regulatory authority also offers guidance and subjects licensed companies to checks and controls at a number of levels, for example planning, operations and customer service. In such a system, legal authority for issuing appropriate guidelines, codes and standards must be devolved to the regulatory body. For instance, a regulatory authority in the energy sector may thereby be permitted to perform the following actions:

- Divide the regulatory task into manageable segments
- Regulate purchase, distribution, supply and utilization of infrastructure services (e.g. electricity and gas)
- Issue licenses for generation, transmission, distribution and supply of electricity and transportation and supply of gas and regulate licensed companies
- Regulate tariffs
- Identify problems that may appear
- Monitor standards and performance

A regulatory authority should be responsible for approving codes and standards applicable to the infrastructure services industry (e.g. electricity supply). In doing so, the authority would aim to ensure the following:

- The scope of codes and standards is adequate to accomplish the task at hand
- Standards are not unduly demanding or unduly lax but appropriate for the price of the service
- Standards and codes are enforced
- Consumers are kept aware of their rights (the authority should do its utmost to ensure that such rights are fulfilled)

All consumers can access affordable and high-quality services

The following six interrelated aspects of regulatory governance (at least) are essential to the development of an effective regulatory framework:

1. Clarity of roles and objectives
2. Autonomy
3. Accountability

Box 2 (continued)

4. Participation
5. Transparency
6. Predictability

The first three aspects relate to the formal legal requirements of regulation and the other criteria relate more closely to informal aspects of regulatory accountability. Whatever the institutional arrangements, the acceptability of a utility regulatory system will depend on all parties (e.g. consumers and private and public sector service providers) understanding the rules of the game (i.e. the principles underpinning utility regulation). This requires regulators to observe the spirit as well as the letter of legislation. It also requires regulators to justify and publicize the reasons for their decisions and approaches and any changes in methodology or procedures.

Africa ranks low in regulatory independence

Most African States rank low in regulatory independence across all sectors and standard international models of infrastructure regulation are not regularly employed in Africa (Gassner and Pushak, 2014, and Wren-Lewis, 2014). Most African regulatory bodies are at an early stage of development, have modest budgets (ranging from less than $300,000 to about $3,000,000 for electricity) and often lack qualified staff members (Vagliasindi and Nellis, 2009, and UNCTAD, 2014b). Staffing levels also vary widely, from one or two to over 30 staff members (UNCTAD, 2014c). This reinforces the need for independent regulatory authorities that are autonomous but also have some political backing to fulfil their roles. In some instances, national bodies need to be bolstered through partnerships and collaboration with regional and pan-territorial regulatory bodies, as they emerge. This could help national bodies, as they may use regional regulatory bodies as a counterweight to domestic political pressures on regulatory governance. There may also be a need to separate supervisory functions (e.g. with regard to competition) from regulatory functions (e.g. price and universal service regulation) to ensure that there is no conflict of interest.

The most prevalent forms of private investment in Africa's infrastructure services sector are in telecommunications — a fast growing sector with relatively high returns on investment — and accounted for 74 per cent of private investment in infrastructure during the period 1990–2013 (African Development Bank, 2014). Table 8 shows the significant differences in the level and form of private participation in infrastructure services in Africa. In the energy sector (primarily electricity, as it accounts for 96 per cent of projects in the sector), the majority of private investment was in greenfield projects. During the period, independent power producers implemented build–own–operate and build–operate–transfer contracts. In contrast, in the water and sewage sector, most private investment projects involved management and lease contracts, but accounted for only 15 per cent of the total amount invested. These differences reflect both the technological characteristics of each sector and the respective market structures. For countries seeking to introduce greater competition into infrastructure services markets, these factors are important in developing a regulatory regime appropriate to the structural characteristics of a given infrastructure services sector (Brown et al., 2006).

In Africa, there has been a relatively high frequency of discontinuation of private sector involvement in the provision of infrastructure services (particularly water). According to one study, 25 per cent of water contracts and 15 per cent of electricity contracts were cancelled during the period 1990–2009, even when performance was judged to have improved (African Development Bank, 2014). In general, there is little empirical consensus on the impact of privatization in developing countries, especially in terms of the relative performance of the private and public sector in infrastructure services provision (Estache and Wodon, 2014; Vagliasindi and Nellis, 2009; and Zhang, 2006).

Although most studies suggest that competition is generally more important than ownership, other factors should also be taken into account in explaining performance improvements in developing countries, such as the quality of institutions and regulation, the existence of well-developed capital markets and private property rights (Pollitt, 1997; Stern and Davis, 1998; and Hare and Davis, 2006). However, the type of infrastructure matters; telecommunications and the majority of energy supply (e.g. generation and distribution) are more amenable to privatization with the introduction of competition than a market for water services, which is usually cost inefficient in most developing countries (UNCTAD, 2014b; and UNCTAD, 2014c). Given the scale of investment in fixed assets or network assets required to supply water, competition is often infeasible (although there is a vibrant water market in a few countries, such as Nigeria) and the costs are high in developing countries.

The Africa Infrastructure Country Diagnostic study collected data measuring institutional reforms in infrastructure undertaken by African countries, utilizing an institutional scorecard comprised of the following three broad areas: reform (sectoral legislation, restructuring of enterprises and private sector participation); regulation (transparent and independent regulatory bodies and tools); and governance (internal management in infrastructure enterprises, such as shareholder relations). Each indicator serves as a basis for measuring the (aggregate and disaggregate)

Table 8. Total public-private partnership infrastructure projects by service sector and type, 1990–2013

Primary sector	Type of public-private partnership	Number of projects	Total investment (million $)
Energy	Concession	19	2 469
	Divestiture	9	1 717
	Greenfield	118	18 205
	Management and lease	18	5
	Total	*164*	*22 396*
Telecommunications	Divestiture	32	23 558
	Greenfield	169	85 174
	Management and lease	4	0
	Total	*205*	*108 732*
Transport	Concession	63	7 782
	Divestiture	3	169
	Greenfield	20	10 237
	Management and lease	16	52
	Total	*102*	*18 241*
Water and sewage	Concession	2	76
	Greenfield	3	259
	Management and lease	23	57
	Total	*28*	*392*
	Grand total	*499*	*149 761*

Source: African Development Bank, 2014.
Note: Most infrastructure projects with private participation fit in one of the above four types, but boundaries between types are not always clear and some projects have features of more than one type. In such instances, projects are classified under the type that better reflects the risks borne by the private sector.

effects of progress in reforms and enterprise performance (Foster and Briceño Garmendia, eds., 2010, and Vagliasindi and Nellis, 2009). The study shows that most African countries have not made progress in these three areas although, in general, institutional development in utilities (ICT, water and energy) is further advanced than in the transport sector (Escribano et al., 2010).

Regional transport and power pool infrastructure have the potential for integration and growth

In Africa, regional infrastructure, such as transport corridors and utility power pools, has the potential for greater integration and widening access to infrastructure services due to economies of scale. National Governments may also induce greater competition between national power producers, though this depends on whether they ease controls on access to distribution networks (Wren-Lewis, 2014). One study estimates returns to cross-border transmission investment of 120 per cent in the Southern African Power Pool and 20 to 30 per cent in other power African pools (Eberhard et al., 2011). However, many countries still need to harmonize their regulatory standards and more effectively pool their resources if this potential is to be realized. In this regard, the Programme for Infrastructure Development in Africa, which merges all continental initiatives on infrastructure, is a useful step forward in trying to pursue greater harmonization.

C. REFORMING INFRASTRUCTURE SERVICES PROVISION IN AFRICA

African Union efforts to prioritize increasing investments and efficiency in the infrastructure services sector can help African countries lay the foundations for future growth. The determination of the optimal policy framework and respective roles of the private and public sectors can only be made nationally. Given the capital-intensive nature of infrastructure provision, due to constrained public finances, African Governments must consider options that encourage private investment where feasible, such as targeted finance aimed at redressing market failures, in the form of equity (e.g. under the Commonwealth Development Corporation) or as long-term loans (e.g. under the Emerging Africa Infrastructure Fund). There are significant in-country investments (e.g. savings and pension funds) not currently tapped for the financing of infrastructure, mainly due to inadequate risk–return ratios and the lack of adequate risk-mitigation mechanisms.

If a country decides to open up the infrastructure services sector, then establishing an institutional framework conducive to promoting competition and governing access, affordability and quality control is an essential prerequisite to privatizing infrastructure services, and policy sequencing and institutional development are therefore important. Critically, policymakers in Africa need to continue their efforts to develop an appropriate legal and regulatory framework for infrastructure services, to encourage investment and improve efficiency in the sector. Domestic regulation should be addressed first, in order that countries do not lose their regulatory policy space in the drive for greater liberalization and attraction of FDI through free trade agreements and bilateral investment treaties.

For African countries with limited experience of the economic regulation of infrastructure services there are few useful examples of how to transition from initial arrangements (e.g. on subsidies and regulatory risk guarantees) to consistency between regulatory legislation and contractual arrangements and to an effective independent regulatory body. Given the heterogeneity of institutional quality and economic development in Africa, it is difficult to directly apply particular country examples in other countries. The example from Uganda in box 3 highlights some elements of regulatory best practice.

Countries also need to improve the capacity-building efforts of regulatory bodies with regard to human resources, to enhance performance, which may be supported regionally through shared training programmes, twinning arrangements and information sharing arrangements to more effectively disseminate best practices and benchmark regulatory performance.

Cross-country regulation, at the regional economic community level or more broadly, is of particular importance. A key issue in such regulation is the harmonization

---

Box 3. Uganda: Best practice in electricity industry regulation

The Ministry of Energy and Mineral Development is responsible for overall management, policy formulation and monitoring of the energy sector in Uganda. The Electricity Regulatory Authority is responsible for the electricity sector. Authority members are appointed by the minister responsible for energy on approval of the cabinet for a period of five years. The Authority is financed by the Ministry of Finance, Planning and Economic Development, by fees prescribed by the Authority on licensing and by a levy not exceeding 0.3 per cent of the revenue generated from the sale of electrical energy. The Authority is independent in the performance of its functions and duties and is not subject to the direction of any person or authority. It is a competent and well-managed regulatory body operating under a well-designed legal framework. The Electricity Regulatory Authority of Uganda provides an effective framework for the support of commercialization and use of private investment in the electricity industry. In addition, the Authority successfully combines concession agreements with the economic regulation of electricity distribution, along with the Ugandan Rural Electrification Fund, to increase electrification rates. The Authority has also made use of a World Bank Partial (regulatory) Risk Guarantee facility to support the concessions and the regulator for the first seven years of the distribution contract.

Source: (UNCTAD, 2014d).

of national standards and systems, to enable linking and coordination of national infrastructure networks. This is crucial for international trade in infrastructure services at regional and global levels. Commitments made through regional trade agreements can also facilitate a process of domestic regulatory reform through the following: widening the scope of competition in services markets to include foreign operators, which could lead to higher output and employment across the sector (as in telecommunications); undertaking commitments to open up services, which may enhance the credibility of domestic policy reforms, as regional commitments can indemnify investors against the risk of possible future policy reversals; and allowing countries to tap into the regulatory expertise of their trading partners, thereby bolstering domestic regulatory capacity and harmonization. Examples of pan-territorial cooperation already in place among regulators include the mechanism for central bankers in Africa, Southern African Development Community (SADC) payment systems, power pools and civil aviation authorities (Páez, 2008a).

Although the State remains a major player in the provision of infrastructure services in Africa, regulatory independence is an important element of effective infrastructure services provision. The type of ownership – whether State, private, public–private partnership or joint venture – may vary, as long as it contributes to a Government's development objectives. Private operation of a State-owned utility is a widely used method in developing countries, as the private sector often considers this less risky than full privatization. Private participation can accelerate infrastructure development and access to improved services. However, Governments must carefully analyse risks, social benefits and employment opportunities.

This chapter discusses critical issues pertaining to the regulation of infrastructure services. In conclusion, given critical infrastructure needs in Africa and the status of infrastructure regulation, African countries may capitalize on opportunities for growth through international trade much more effectively if regulation addresses some of the infrastructure services constraints currently faced in Africa. This requires innovative policy reforms aimed at improving the institutional relevance and performance of regulatory bodies tasked with the mandate of balancing fiscal, national, public and private demands. For African firms to effectively exploit growing opportunities for expanded trade through global services value chains, major investments in transport, logistics and energy infrastructure are required.

CHAPTER 3

ADDRESSING THE POLICY DISCONNECT IN AFRICA'S SERVICES TRADE

A. INTRODUCTION

A review of economic trends, the contribution of services to the economy (chapter 1), and critical regulatory policy issues concerning the services sector (chapter 2) is followed by a discussion of the policy dimension of services trade. To assess the extent to which services trade forms part of Africa's development strategies, this chapter undertakes a non-exhaustive mapping exercise of existing policies that pertain to services trade at the national, regional and global levels to determine how well such policies reflect the potential contribution of the sector to overarching development goals of African Governments. The chapter concludes with a discussion of the policy disconnect between existing national, regional and global policies that pertain to services trade and offers recommendations as to how African countries, regional economic communities and the African Union can bridge this divide so that such trade can be better harnessed to address inclusive growth and economic development priorities on the continent.

B. MAPPING AFRICAN SERVICES POLICIES AT THE NATIONAL LEVEL

The most important policy document providing a vision and strategy for development is a national development plan in which development priorities, including sectors, are spelled out. Many African countries have one. Given the relevance of the services trade, mapping how it is treated in the context of national development plans can be revealing in terms of policy relevance and the extent to which services trade has been mainstreamed into a national development vision.

In a non-exhaustive mapping exercise conducted for this report, national development plans of 38 African countries were reviewed. Four central questions were asked to assess the extent to which the services sector is viewed as a conduit for achieving a country's national development objectives:

a) Are services mentioned in the national development plan?

b) Is services trade or liberalization mentioned?

c) Is there a link between services and national development goals?

d) Are services linked to a regional development strategy?

Figure 5 captures the results of the mapping exercise of the 38 national development plans reviewed. It shows that services are considered important for development by most African countries. It also indicates that the 38 countries reviewed mention services in their development plans and that they link services to national development goals. Services trade is also perceived as important by African countries, since 37 of the 38 included services trade in their development plans. However, regional integration does not appear to be equally prioritized, as only 13 countries of the sample linked services to this element.

Although most of the reviewed countries mention services trade or services liberalization in their national development plans, there are significant differences among these countries as to how services trade is to be promoted and/or developed in these plans. For example, a limited number of countries mention services trade explicitly; however, most only mention it with regard to certain sectors. Some countries, such as the Congo, Botswana, Cameroon, Rwanda and South Africa, include more elaborate narratives on services trade, highlighting its importance and describing how it can contribute to development. For instance, the National Development Plan 2030 of South Africa envisions trade in services as a means to move towards faster growth. In particular, it identifies finance and

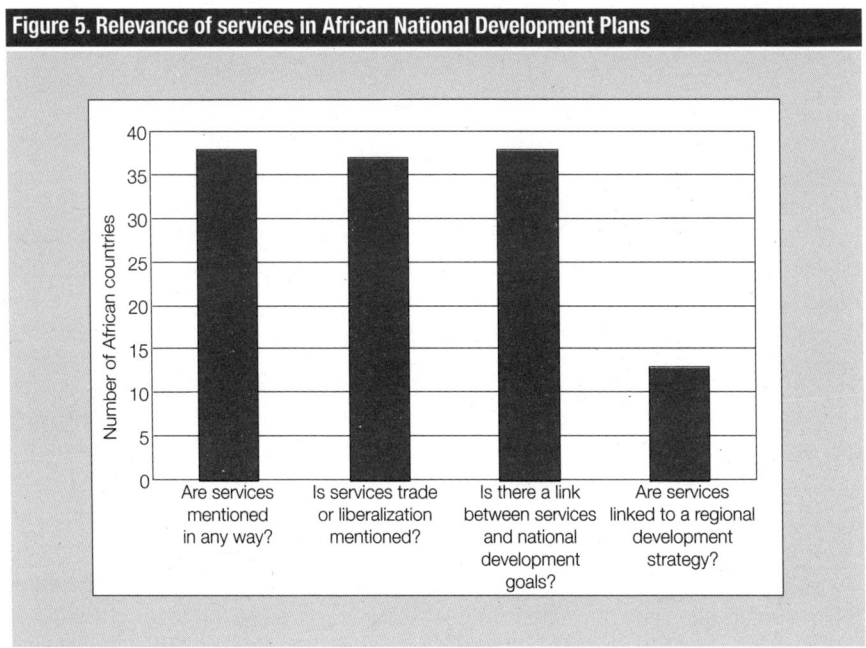

Figure 5. Relevance of services in African National Development Plans

Source: UNCTAD secretariat.

business services, tourism and higher education as priority sectors for South Africa. The Plan explains how increased exports in these sectors are expected to lead to increased growth, which will be necessary to achieve economic transformation and create employment.

Several of the above-mentioned countries also highlight the relevance of business process outsourcing services as having the potential to boost services exports and create employment. For instance, the tenth national development plan of Botswana identifies its comparative advantage in services — for example, routine administration, data inputting and simple data analysis — that could use relatively abundant low-skilled labour. Similarly, Cameroon intends to make use of its educated youth to attract international companies providing services such as call centres, software engineering, distance data processing and telemedicine. The aim is to turn Cameroon into a net exporter of services.

Similarly, the Economic Development and Poverty Reduction Strategy 2013–2018 of Rwanda considers business process outsourcing to be a means of generating youth employment opportunities. The strategy provides for export-oriented investment in financial services that would enable Rwanda to become an attractive financial services centre in the region.

Other than these few examples, most of the national development plans do not clearly address trade in services broadly, but prioritize certain services sectors where it is implicitly part of the sector. For example, tourism is considered a key sector in many of the plans under this category. Cabo Verde, the Comoros, Ghana, Kenya, Lesotho and the Seychelles all identify tourism as a key sector in their national development plans. Another sector where trade in services frequently occurs in the reviewed plans is the transport sector, when there is a cross-border element. For example, Namibia's Fourth National Development Plan cites logistics as one of four economic priorities and aims for the country to become a regional transport hub.

While trade in services and a link between services and development were mentioned in the development plans of many of the reviewed African countries, significantly fewer countries linked services to regional development strategies. Thirteen of the 38 countries reviewed included this particular dimension. The national development plans of some countries — Botswana, Kenya, Rwanda and Burundi — provide a relatively detailed account of policies dealing with aspects of regional integration and make specific references to regional economic communities and their legislation. For instance, Kenya mentions the promotion of East African

Community (EAC) financial services integration to facilitate trade and cross-border operations, and the movement of capital is one of the measures mentioned in its national development plan. The Rwandan national development plan also makes a link between regional integration and services sectors. For instance, Rwanda's policy to improve the free movement of skilled labour is regarded as important, as it has successfully attracted skilled labour to sectors such as finance and professional services. In this respect, the Plan refers to the EAC Common Market and the rules providing for the free movement of labour within EAC and provisions on free trade in services, which allows services providers to set up in other EAC member States.

Some development plans address regional integration with regard to services, services sectors or the extension of markets for services, without referring to particular protocols relating to regional economic communities. One example is the development plan of Lesotho, which recognizes the need for the country to take advantage of regional markets such as the Southern African Customs Union and SADC, owing to its small domestic market for services exports, among other reasons. In some instances regional integration is linked to one or more services sectors, as is the case in the national development plan of Cabo Verde, which strives for regional integration in the air transportation subsector. Similarly, Guinea, Liberia and Nigeria mention a regional transit and transport facilitation initiative by the Economic Community of West African States (ECOWAS) in their development plans.

C. MAPPING AFRICAN SERVICES POLICIES AT THE REGIONAL LEVEL

Regional economic communities are making modest but steady progress in services trade liberalization.

Since the promulgation of the Abuja Treaty in 1991, Africa has been making important strides in regional integration. Most of the regional economic communities, which form the pillars of regional integration in Africa, have made steady progress towards the creation of free trade areas and customs unions.[5] These efforts, together with the recently launched initiative for the creation of a CFTA, are key milestones towards the consolidation of the African Economic Community, as envisioned in the Abuja Treaty.

The Community would constitute a pan-African economic space where goods, people, capital and notably services move freely. To date, emphasis in the regional economic communities has been placed primarily on liberalizing trade in goods — and to some degree, the movement of persons — while less attention has been given to the services sector. Indeed, at the level of the regional economic communities, greater progress has been made in the development of protocols that cater for trade in goods. The total elimination of tariffs on goods is foreseen in virtually all of the regional economic communities.

In contrast, the opening up of services trade in the African regional context has been more gradual. This is partly because of the complexity of services trade negotiations, which require agreeing on a common set of rules to regulate the sector, but also due to the intrinsic nature of trade in services. To ensure adequate market access, domestic regulation often needs to be revised and reformed so that foreign services providers are not discriminated against. Given these intrinsic complexities, African countries in their respective subregions have preferred a more gradual approach through either sectoral or modal[6] regulation. A case in point is the sectoral approach to transport and telecommunications that has been developed in the ECOWAS and SADC regions, as well as regulations pertaining to the free movement of persons which takes a modal approach in COMESA, ECOWAS and SADC.

In recent years, member States have prioritized the need for deepening these commitments, recognizing that services trade forms part of the integration agenda leading up to the African Economic Community. More importantly, many African Governments have come to realize the importance of the services economy in Africa's growth story and the role the sector can play in sustainable livelihoods and poverty reduction. This heightened relevance of the services sector has gained momentum, and African countries are trying to harness the development of services trade through the promulgation of regional protocols targeting the services sector more comprehensively.

To illustrate this regional trend, table 9 outlines the main regional instruments at the regional economic community level dealing with trade in services, their major principles and policies, and the institutional framework governing them. At a glance, there are numerous instruments with varying degrees of coverage and differing approaches for treating trade in services. First, there are instruments covering all, or at least several, services sectors, with comprehensive rules that are applied across these sectors. This is a horizontal approach. Second, there are instruments with a much narrower scope, focusing exclusively on one services sector or subsector and containing provisions that apply solely to that particular sector. This is a sectoral approach. Third, some instruments deal with a particular mode of delivery, such as the movement of natural persons or commercial presence of the service provider, hence a modal approach.

While some regions have made a head start on comprehensive across-the-board services liberalization, others have tended to focus more on specific modes of delivery or subsectors or used a combination of these approaches. For example, COMESA, EAC and SADC are at the forefront of promoting services trade in their respective subregions. Each of these regional economic communities has a protocol in place that caters for comprehensive services liberalization across various services sectors.[7]

The members of these three regional economic communities are also currently involved in negotiations to establish a joint free trade area known as the COMESA–EAC–SADC tripartite free trade area, which would comprise 26 member countries constituting a market over 600 million people and a combined GDP of $1 trillion. The tripartite also envisages services liberalization in a second phase of negotiations, after having extensively negotiated trade in goods in phase 1 during 2014. It is expected that modalities for services negotiations in phase 2 will build on the protocols of these regional economic communities and the negotiating experience with these instruments (COMESA, 2014; International Centre for Trade and Sustainable Development, 2014).

From a sectoral perspective, several regional economic communities are engaged in developing regional regulatory and policy instruments pertaining to one or more of the services subsectors. For example, ECOWAS and SADC have made progress in regulating telecommunications, while the Economic Community of Central African States has focused on the transport and communications sector, and the Intergovernmental Authority on Development has addressed the tourism sector through a master plan on sustainable tourism (Economic Commission for Africa, 2013). The promulgation of sectoral regulation also reflects the shared approach within regional economic communities to prioritize and cooperate in those sectors that are critical in overcoming infrastructure and supply side constraints faced by trade.

From a modal perspective, regulation in some regional economic communities caters for the free movement of natural persons (mode 4) (see, for example, the COMESA Framework for Liberalizing Trade in Services). As shown in table 9,

Table 9. Major instruments, policies and institutions dealing with services issues in regional economic communities

Regional economic communities	Treaties, agreements or instruments	Major principles and policies	Institutional framework
Arab Maghreb Union	Constitutive Treaty of the Arab Maghreb Union (1989)	Art. 2 envisages the free movement of persons and transfer of services, goods and capital in the region.	Presidential Council of the Union
	Convention on the encouragement and protection of investments between the countries of the Union (1993)	Countries are encouraged to liberalize their investment, to exempt tariffs and registration fees on investment of the region, and to extend fiscal benefits accorded to foreign investors	
Community of Sahelo-Saharan States	Treaty establishing the Community of Sahelo-Saharan States (1998)	Art. 2 foresees the elimination of obstacles impeding the unity of its member States by adopting measures that allow freedom of movement of individuals, national goods, merchandise and services. Transport is highlighted as a priority sector. Improvement of land, air and sea transport and telecommunications among its members and the implementation of joint projects are key objectives.	Council of Heads of State and Executive Council of the Community
	COMESA Treaty (1994)	Art. 4 mandates the removal of obstacles to the free movement of services and capital within COMESA. It also envisages cooperation in certain services sectors, namely transport, communications, tourism and health. Art. 164 mandates the conclusion of a protocol on the movement of persons to supersede the existing 1984 protocol.	The Authority
	COMESA Framework for liberalizing trade in services (2004)	Art. 3 seeks to liberalize trade in services beyond the depth and scope of GATS, with a view to creating a single market for trade in services. Annex I envisages negotiations of specific commitments for the free movement of persons.	Committee on Trade in Services
COMESA	Protocol on the Free Movement of Persons, Labour, Services, Rights of Establishment and Residence (2001)	To supersede the 1984 protocol upon entry into force. Art. 2 envisages the gradual removal of restrictions on the free movement of persons and the right to take up employment, manage companies and reside in any member State.	Council of the Common Market
	Protocol on the Gradual Relaxation and Eventual Elimination of Visas (1984)	Provides for the dismantling of obstacles to the movement of persons, in particular visa requirements, within COMESA.	
	Investment Agreement for the COMESA Common Investment Area (2007)	Applies to investments of COMESA investors who have been registered in the member State in which the investment is made. COMESA investors can hire qualified persons from any country, giving priority to qualified workers from member States with equal qualifications.	COMESA Common Investment Area Committee

Table 9 (contd.)

Regional economic communities	Treaties, agreements or instruments	Major principles and policies	Institutional framework
East African Community Common Market	Protocol Establishing the Common Market (2009)	Art. 4(2) mentions as an objective the acceleration of economic growth and development of partner States by attaining the free movement of goods, persons, services and capital. Parts D and E of the protocol deal with the free movement of persons and the right of establishment and residence. Part F deals with the free movement of services, and Part G provides for the free movement of capital. Annex V contains a schedule of commitments of services liberalization.	Council of Ministers of the Community
Economic Community of Central African States	Treaty Establishing the Economic Community of Central African States (1983)	Art. 4 aims to progressively abolish obstacles between members to the free movement of persons, goods, services and capital and to the right of establishment. Cooperation in certain services sectors covers transport and communication, education, training and culture, and tourism. Relevant protocols for each of these sectors form part of the Treaty.	Conference of Heads of State and Government
	Revised Treaty of the Economic Community of West African States (1993)	Art. 3 of the Treaty looks at the harmonization and coordination of national policies and the promotion of integration programmes and projects, including services. It also envisages the removal of obstacles to the free movement of persons, services and capital, and to the right of residence and establishment. Arts. 32–34 also make special mention of three services sectors: transport, postal and telecommunications, and tourism.	Authority of Heads of State and Government
ECOWAS	Protocol and supplementary protocols on free movement of persons, right of residence and establishment (1979–1990)	The Protocol guarantees nationals of ECOWAS States the right to enter, reside and establish economic activities in the territory of member States, and sets out the elimination of restrictions on these rights in three phases. Subsequent legislation has eliminated visa restrictions, recognizes property rights and norms the establishment and access to enterprises in the Community.	Council of Ministers
	Supplementary Act on Universal Access/ Service for Telecommunications (2007)	The Act regulates the access to telecommunication networks, as well as policy design at community level, to ensure universal access and governs the participation of the private sector.	ECOWAS Ministerial Monitoring Committee
	ECOWAS Supplementary Act on Common Investment Market (2008)	Covers all investments made by an investor before or after entry into force, provided that an investor is an individual or company of a member State of ECOWAS, or a company that has invested or is making an investment in the territory of an ECOWAS member.	

Table 9 (contd.)

Regional economic communities	Treaties, agreements or instruments	Major principles and policies	Institutional framework
Inter governmental Authority on Development	Agreement Establishing the Intergovernmental Authority on Development (1996)	Art. 7 seeks to harmonize policies on trade, transport and communications, and promote the free movement of services in the region. Elements of services are further addressed in creating an enabling environment for foreign, cross-border and domestic trade and investment, and developing and improving transport infrastructure.	Assembly of Heads of State and Government
	Sustainable Tourism Master Plan for the Inter-governmental Authority on Development (IGAD) Region (2013)	The main objective is to provide a regional framework for sustainable tourism that contributes to socioeconomic development and poverty alleviation. The priority areas of the Plan are policy, regulatory and institutional framework, tourism product development, tourism marketing, human resource development, research and development, investment in tourism infrastructure, infrastructure development, and tourism and natural and cultural heritage conservation.	Tourism Commission, member States and regional tourism stakeholders of the Authority
	Protocol on Trade in Services (2012)	Art. 2 seeks to progressively liberalize intraregional trade in services to create a single market.	Committee of Ministers responsible for trade matters
	Protocol on the facilitation of movement of persons (2005)	Art. 2 lays out as overall objective the development of policies which target the progressive elimination of obstacles to the movement of persons in the SADC region).	Population registries of SADC member States
Southern African Development Authority	Protocol on Transport, Communications and Metrology (1996)	Art. 2.4 envisages the integration of regional transport, communications and meteorology networks to be facilitated by the implementation of compatible policies, legislation, rules, standards and procedures; and the elimination or reduction of barriers to the movement of persons, goods, equipment and services. Covers all transport, telecommunications and postal services.	Southern Africa Transport and Communications Commission
		Art. 2 envisages tourism as a vehicle for the social and economic development of SADC. Seeks to facilitate intraregional travel by removing travel and visa restrictions to develop tourism	
	Protocol on the Development of Tourism in the (1998)		SADC Committee of Tourism Ministers

Sources: UNCTAD, extracted from the legal texts cited under column 2.

relevant progress has been made in the implementation of some of these regional instruments. This is true with regard to ECOWAS and EAC, where the citizens of those countries have community passports allowing them to travel and work within their respective regions. Important milestones relate to the elimination of visa requirements for short-term stays, recognition and accreditation of professional qualifications, and authorization to buy property and establish business operations.

Indeed, the movement of persons has been the element of services trade that has advanced at the fastest pace relative to other modes of supply. This has been supported by various developments. First, the vision enshrined in the Abuja Treaty of the African Economic Community, where African nationals should be free to travel across the continent without restrictions, is clearly formulated and consistently reflected in all the treaties of regional economic communities. Second, it is also explained by the modal nature of business in Africa, which has been historically characterized by traders crossing porous borders and supported by the notion that it is essential for business people, transporters and tourists to be able to cross borders freely in order to foster intraregional trade. Third, progress in transport facilitation at a regional level, such as improved customization and standardized border controls for vehicles, has greatly supported the realization of the movement of persons.

An important indicator of such progress is the development of an increasingly mobile labour market that is expanding regionally, supported by a high demand for professional services (Dihel et al., 2005). In this regard, an important EAC milestone is the elimination of restrictions on the ability of legal professionals to work in Kenya, Rwanda, Uganda and the United Republic of Tanzania. Regional integration is also helping build up the professional labour force as students of the tertiary sector are increasingly able to access educational services across borders (African Union, 2014a; Herrmann, 2012).

Nonetheless, the sector is still hampered by restrictions, and regional commitments take time to materialize at the national level. For example, the COMESA Protocol on the Free Movement of Persons, Labour, Services, the Right of Establishment and Residence (2001) was signed only by four member States and ratified by one country, which explains why operationalization of this protocol may take longer in a 20-country region. In contrast, the Protocol on the Gradual Relaxation and Eventual Elimination of Visas (1984) was signed and ratified by 17 countries (COMESA, 2014). Beyond ratification, the operationalization of policy comprises a number of steps that often need to be accompanied by the adoption of a legal instrument that domesticates the policy at a national level. This may require the engagement of parliament. Subsequently, efforts may also include the internalization of the instrument at various government levels. The implementation process generally entails considerable human and financial resources.

Further, professional qualifications are subject to varying degrees of recognition and accreditation requirements. This affects modal access to services trade, as they de facto restrict access to the labour market for foreign providers of certain professionals such as accountants, attorneys and physicians. Lastly, countries may also fail to comply with regional regulation because of security, safety and health concerns. This is true of the recent Ebola outbreak, which has severely hampered the movement of persons in affected regions.

Finally, as shown in table 9, some regional economic communities (COMESA, ECOWAS, SADC and the Arab Maghreb Union) have also endorsed finance and investment regulations. After an overview of existing regulations and policies pertaining to the services sector across the regional economic communities, it is necessary to take a closer look at the scope and coverage of such regulation. The level and breadth covered across the different regional economic communities varies; however, some important commonalities may be distilled from the more progressive protocols in COMESA, EAC and SADC. The main legal elements of these instruments are described in table 10 below.

For example, the services protocols of COMESA, EAC and SADC cover services that are supplied by service providers that are nationals (either natural or juridical persons) of the partner States. The protocols do not cover services that are being supplied in the exercise of government authority — that is to say, public services — which is also consistent with GATS. Equally, the scope of these instruments is far reaching in terms of services sectors, though not as comprehensive as GATS, which covers 12 services sectors. In comparison, COMESA members have identified four priority sectors, EAC members, seven sectors; and SADC, six. Across the range of selected sectors, the protocols of all three regional economic communities cover finance, transport, communication and tourism, which are critical enabling services for trade in goods, and if properly liberalized, could significantly boost intraregional trade in Eastern and Southern Africa.

In the three regional economic communities, most-favoured nation treatment (MFN) is offered to service providers horizontally, across the selected services sectors. Further, the standard of treatment in the three protocols is no less favourable treatment, which ensures that service providers within the regional economic communities are given at least the same preferences as foreign providers covered in the context of other free trade areas. This ensures that any preferential treatment that a party to the regional economic community may have conferred or will confer to a third party will be automatically extended to service providers within the regional economic community. It does not however, deal with the second dimension of discrimination, which relates to the type of treatment a foreign services provider receives compared with a national service provider. This second dimension of discrimination is normally covered by national treatment, which ensures that foreign and domestic service providers within the regional economic communities will receive like treatment. In the case of COMESA and SADC instruments, only MFN is offered to the services sectors covered by their respective protocols, whereas the EAC instrument also offers national treatment. Hence, it could be argued that the former two instruments are slightly more restrictive than the latter, given that service providers within the regional economic communities may still face stiff competition from national providers.

Rules of origin and admission requirements covering the movement of natural persons are also treated differently in the protocols. COMESA spells out mode 4 commitments in its schedule of commitments and in the Protocol on the Free Movement of Persons, Labour, Services, the Right of Establishment and Residence. A similar approach is employed by EAC; however, the SADC Protocol does not cover the movement of natural persons; hence foreign providers do not enjoy market access.

COMESA, EAC and SADC member States waived the obligations to confer preferential treatment to service providers in the regional economic communities under special circumstances, according to the reservations and exceptions provisions contained in their respective protocols. Standard exceptions in the three protocols pertain to disclosing information that may compromise public interest or health, safety or public moral consideration. This corresponds with standard general exceptions in GATS article XIV.

An important difference across the three protocols is how disputes arising from the violation or interpretation of these instruments are treated. COMESA and SADC refer such cases to their respective tribunals, provided consultation (and mediation in the case of SADC) has been exhausted. These are standard mechanisms in many existing free trade areas today. In contrast, EAC refers exclusively to the exhaustion of local remedies, which means seeking legal redress through national courts in EAC countries.

Performance requirements relate to the establishment of quotas or ceilings to the quantity, volume or value of the services rendered. The EAC Protocol is silent on performance requirements. This makes it the least restrictive of the three instruments. In contrast, both the COMESA and SADC instruments do provide for performance requirements. For COMESA, these come in the form of economic needs tests and quantitative restrictions inscribed in annexes I and III of its two protocols.

All three instruments also have standard notification requirements requiring members to promptly publish any regulation pertaining to trade in services, including the signing of international agreements. This requirement is important and mirrors the notification requirement of GATS article V, in particular when it comes to international agreements that may confer MFN treatment to third country services operators and hence dilute the preferences of the service providers from the region.

Finally, all three instruments also envisage progressive services liberalization through sequential trade negotiation rounds, which implies that barriers to trade in services will be dismantled over time. In practice, however, these rounds have been difficult to accomplish, in particular for SADC, which has not yet completed its first round, and COMESA, which is in the process of negotiating the schedule of commitments in the four identified priority sectors (COMESA, 2014).

It is expected that services negotiations in the tripartite free trade area will build on existing regulation at the level of the regional economic communities. Some of the common elements in the treatment of services trade highlighted in this analysis could serve as a basis for negotiations. It is likely that the 26 members of the tripartite agree on binding existing levels of liberalization in the schedules of commitments of each of the regional economic communities and to leave progressive liberalization for future rounds. However, if the outcome of the tripartite is to be ambitious, member States could push beyond retaining the status quo and make deeper commitments than heretofore. Much will depend on the modalities that are sketched out for the second phase of negotiations, and, given the measured progress made on issues such as rules of origin, the tripartite members may converge toward a more modest agreement on services.

The services trade agenda is starting to gain ground at a pan-African level.

There have also been some recent initiatives at the pan-African level to incorporate trade in services as part of a wider African Union agenda towards the realization of the African Economic Community. An African Union decision (Assembly/AU/

Dec.394(XVIII) and declaration (Assembly/AU/Decl.1(XVIII)) on boosting intra-African trade, adopted in 2012, are also steps forward. Emanating from the decision are two core documents, the Action plan for boosting intra-African trade and the Framework, road map and architecture for fast-tracking the establishment of a continental free trade area, which are blueprints deemed to instrumentalize a CFTA by 2017. Services trade is not prioritized in both instruments, as they deal mainly with trade in goods. However, it is partly addressed in these instruments, and an incorporated agenda is likely to be developed for services trade as the action plan and road map and architecture are operationalized.

For example, the action plan revolves around seven priority clusters, which have built-in targets[8] that are aligned to existing milestones and objectives under the Accelerated Industrial Development of Africa action plan, the Minimum Integration Programme and the Programme for Infrastructure Development in Africa. These clusters focus on the following areas:

a) Trade policy;

b) Trade facilitation;

c) Productive capacity;

d) Trade-related infrastructure;

e) Trade finance;

f) Trade information;

g) Factor market integration.

As services trade does not form a cluster in itself, elements of trade-enabling services are integrated into some of the seven clusters. For example, in the trade and policy cluster, mention is made of the need to make unilateral commitments to liberalize trade-related services such as transport, professional, financial and ICT services. Equally, financial services, mainly in the form of export credits and guarantees, are embedded in the targets of the trade finance cluster, and both the trade facilitation and trade-related infrastructure clusters have a direct bearing on storage, transport and freight services.

Progress has also been made in some sectoral and modal aspects of services trade at the pan-African level, in particular transport, tourism and modal services, which are conduits for the movement of persons. Important sectoral milestones for the transport sector have been achieved under the Africa Transport Policy Programme, which aims to improve the connectivity of Africa through

Table 10. Legal elements of horizontal services protocols in the regional economic communities

Elements	COMESA	EAC	SADC
Definitions: Services	Services provided by a natural person or juridical entity (art. 2), except services in the exercise of governmental authority (art. 5).	Services supplied by nationals of Partner States. Services in the exercise of government authority are not included (art. 16).	Includes any service in any sector by a service supplier from a State party, except those supplied in the exercise of governmental authority (art. 3).
Scope	Focuses on measures affecting services trade of four priority sectors[a] covering the four modes of supply (art. 5) in a schedule of commitments (annex III).	Focuses on measures affecting services trade of an initial list of seven services sectors[b] covering four modes of supply in a schedule of commitments (annex V).	Focuses on measures applied by States parties that affect trade in services with an initial list of six priority sectors[c] covering the four modes of supply (art. 3).
Treatment	MFN treatment is offered. The standard of treatment is no less favorable treatment than that offered to like service and service suppliers of other countries (art. 6). MFN exemptions are listed in annex II, to be phased out in five years (art. 7). Market access and national treatment are also covered in arts. 26–27, but are limited to the scheduled commitments in Annex III.	MFN and national treatment are offered, and are informed by what is inscribed in the schedules of commitments. The standard of treatment is no less favorable treatment than that offered to like service and service suppliers of other partner States or third countries (arts. 17–18).	MFN treatment is offered, and the standard of treatment is no less favorable treatment than that offered to like service and service suppliers of other partner States or third countries (art. 4). MFN exemptions are listed in annex. Market access and the national treatment are also covered in arts. 14–15, but are limited to the scheduled commitments of the future annex of the protocol upon adoption of the schedules.
Rules of origin and admission requirements	These are spelled out in the schedules of commitments at a sectoral level for each country (annex III) and in annex I of the Protocol on the Free Movement of Natural Persons.	Spelled out in the schedules of commitments at a sectoral level for each country (annex V) and in accordance with the Schedule for the Free Movement of Workers (annex II of the Protocol).	The protocol does not cover measures affecting natural persons seeking employment in the SADC labour market (art.17).
Reservations and exceptions	Art. 9 exempts member States from disclosing confidential information and data that would impede law enforcement or compromise public or particular commercial interests. Art. 21 allows for exceptions to apply measures restricting trade in services for public moral and order, health and safety considerations, among others.	Art. 21 lists situations in which measures that restrict trade in services may be allowed: the protection of public morals, health considerations and safety considerations, and others. Art. 22 spells out exceptions for disclosing information that may compromise security interests.	Art. 10 lists general exceptions such as the protection of public morals and order, health considerations, and safety and security interests. An additional waiver to comply with obligations is found in art. 23. Art. 8 also exempts member States from disclosing any confidential information contrary to public interest.

Table 10 (contd.)

Elements	COMESA	EAC	SADC
Dispute resolution	Art. 29 provides for dispute settlement in the COMESA Court of Justice, provided consultations have been undertaken first.	Art. 54 provides for dispute settlement for disputes arising from the interpretation or application of the protocol through domestic adjudication channels.	Art. 25 provides for dispute settlement procedures in annex 1 of the protocol, providing for consultations, mediation and recourse to the SADC Tribunal.
Performance requirements	Annex I pertains to economic needs tests and quantitative restrictions for mode 4, and art. 26 allows for performance requirements that are inscribed in the annex III schedules.	Not mentioned.	Art. 14 allows for performance requirements that are inscribed in the schedules to be appended to the annex, once the protocol is adopted.
Transparency	Art. 8 requires member States to promptly publish and make publicly available all regulations that pertain to services, including international agreements, by notification to the Secretary-General of COMESA.	Art. 19 sets out notification requirements of all measures affecting the free movement of services, including the signing with third parties of international agreements that pertain to or affect trade in services.	Art. 8 requests State parties to promptly publish and notify any regulations, including international agreements, that affect trade in services. The Trade Negotiating Forum for Services should be informed annually.

Sources: COMESA, 2001, 2004; EAC, 2009; SADC, 2012.
Notes: a Communication, finance, transport and tourism.
b Business services, communication services, distribution services, education services, financial services, tourism and travel related services and transport.
c Communication, construction, energy-related, financial, tourism and transport services.

comprehensive road and transport corridors and networks, in an effort to improve the situation of transporting goods and people across Africa. Other strides include the the Yamoussoukro Decision (2000), which sets milestones for the liberalization of air transport across Africa, and the tourism action plan adopted in 2004 by the African Union and the New Partnership for Africa's Development to promote the tourism sector and its related services, and in turn foster economic development and growth.

Modal aspects of services trade covered at the pan-African level relate to regulation that has been endorsed at heads of State level with a bearing on the movement of persons, such as the migration policy framework for Africa (African Union, 2006a) and the Common African position on migration and development (African Union, 2006b). These pan-African instruments, together with the protocols of the regional economic communities mapped out in the previous section, constitute a prolific body of law and policy on the movement of persons. These are important steps being taken towards the negotiation of the CFTA. It is likely that the modalities for negotiations on mode 4 will build on these achievements, and this should ensure consistency between what regulates migration and the movement of persons at the subregional and pan-African levels. Equally important is the development of pan-African standards to harmonize existing policies on the mutual recognition and accreditation of qualifications so that people moving across borders will have an opportunity to exercise their profession in a future pan-African labour market of the African Economic Community.

Although there has been some important progress at the continental level to bring a regional dimension into services trade, the African Union still lacks a comprehensive services vision document or strategy. To move forward, a major element that should be addressed in preparation for the launch of the CFTA will be modalities that guide negotiations on two fronts: first, the actual content of the CFTA agreement or treaty and accompanying regulation that is specific to the areas covered by the agreement (for example, protocols dealing with trade in goods, rules of origin, non-tariff barriers, services, movement of natural persons), and second, modalities that guide market access negotiations to liberalize each of these areas across the 54 African countries.

The EAC–COMESA–SADC Tripartite Agreement has been marked by difficulties in concluding the first phase of negotiations. The proposed approach to establishing the CFTA, and which forms an integral part of its road map and architecture, is to build on the gains of existing services trade regulation and policy at the level of regional economic communities. However, if African member States wish to have an ambitious outcome of CFTA negotiations, they should support the idea of deeper and progressive liberalization, with commitments targeting services trade at horizontal, sectoral and modal levels from an initial phase, not as a built-in agenda for the future. Whatever the approach, the process towards the establishment of the CFTA is in itself a unique opportunity for African countries to align their existing national, regional and global policies on services trade.

D. MAPPING AFRICA'S SERVICES TRADE POLICIES AT THE GLOBAL LEVEL

African member States have made important services trade liberalization commitments at the global level.

The multilateral trading system is the space in which international business transactions take place and that regulates their orderly functioning. It is a vibrant and expanding system, owing to the relatively recent emergence of a body of international trade law that is predictable, transparent and enforceable. The international organization with the mandate to regulate and oversee the application of rules of this system is WTO.

The multilateral trading system is composed of three regulatory pillars enshrined in the General Agreement on Tariffs and Trade, GATS and the Agreement on Trade-Related Aspects of Intellectual Property Rights. These three agreements govern trade in goods, services and intellectual property, respectively, and with a set of special agreements, they compose a regulatory framework that disciplines trade across 160 countries, including 42 African member States of WTO.

With the adoption of GATS through the Uruguay Round agreements, WTO members have adopted an agenda of progressive services liberalization. All WTO members are bound by the provisions on services contained in GATS, though at differing levels. The degree to which members liberalize their services sectors is defined by their schedules of commitments. Correspondingly, though all of the 42 African countries that are WTO members have inscribed sectoral and/or horizontal commitments in their schedules,[9] the level of liberalization of each country varies considerably.

The schedules of commitments are the blueprint of what WTO members have committed to liberalize. Since GATS follows a positive list approach, it is presumed that what has been inscribed in the schedules forms part of a progressive liberalization agenda and that a subsequent reduction of market access and national treatment restrictions to these services in future trade rounds is to be expected. As stated earlier, there is a high degree of variability across Africa in terms of what has been inscribed, both from a horizontal, sectoral and modal perspective, and this is compounded by the degree of technical difficulty of interpreting a services schedule (WTO, 2001). A schedule is typically composed of three sections: a horizontal section, where limitations that a country may wish to apply to all sectors are included; a sectoral section, which list the sectors the country is willing to liberalize under GATS; and an MFN exemptions section, which carves out the specific conditions under which a country may violate the MFN principle of GATS, and therefore discriminate against a particular or a group of WTO members on a selective basis.

In addition to the current 42 African members of WTO, another 9 African countries are in the process of joining the Organization. This process can span over more than a decade. The entry costs to WTO are high, as countries must develop a schedule of liberalization of commitments for goods and services on a request-offer basis by the existing 160 members. Once this process is completed, it is expected that the new members will adopt the WTO agreements in a single undertaking, meaning they will automatically be bound by the existing provisions on services under GATS, as well as the other WTO agreements.

Table 11 summarizes key commitments across the 42 African countries that are WTO members. The scope and coverage of these schedules portray a high degree of variability across the Africa. That countries can opt into sectors through the positive list approach of GATS renders a high degree of heterogeneity in the liberalization of services across the continent. It also reflects the different priorities countries have and how they position themselves more broadly in the cross-sectoral negotiations of WTO, where other (non-services) priorities may take centre stage.[10]

Of the 42 African countries, 20 have inscribed horizontal commitments, all countries have made sectoral commitments and 17 have MFN exemptions. The content of the schedules ranges from single-sector coverage (Burkina Faso, Chad and Mauritania for tourism and travel-related services; Madagascar for business services), to a full-fledged schedule covering all sectors (the Gambia).

From all the schedules, the sector that is most frequently inscribed is the tourism and travel sector (40 of the 42 African member States have made commitments in this sector), followed by business services (23 countries), and communication

Table 11. Overview of commitments scheduled under the General Agreement on Trade in Services by African member States

Country	Horizontal commitments	*Sectoral commitments* — Business services	Communications services	Construction and related services	Distribution services	Educational services	Environmental services	Financial services	Health-related and social services	Tourism and travel services	Recreational, cultural and sporting services	Transport services	Other services not included elsewhere	*MFN exemptions* — Cross-sectoral services	Business services	Communications services	Construction and related servies	Distribution services	Educational services	Environmental services	Financial services	Health-related and social services	Tourism and travel services	Recreational, cultural and sporting services	Transport services	Other services not included elsewhere
Zimbabwe	•		•						•	•																
Zambia	•	•		•																				•	•	
United Rep. of Tanzania										•																
Uganda		•								•																
Tunisia	•	•						•		•					•		•									•
Togo			•							•	•															
Swaziland	•	•								•	•										•					•
South Africa	•	•	•	•	•		•	•	•	•		•	•								•					•
Sierra Leone	•	•	•	•			•	•	•	•	•	•		•	•	•	•	•		•	•	•	•	•	•	•
Senegal	•	•	•		•				•	•	•	•									•					•
Rwanda	•						•	•		•	•															
Nigeria	•	•							•	•	•															
Niger										•	•														•	
Namibia	•	•								•																
Mozambique								•																		
Morocco	•	•	•	•			•	•		•		•									•					•
Mauritius	•	•						•		•											•					
Mauritania										•																
Mali					•					•															•	
Malawi	•	•		•				•	•	•																
Madagascar	•																									
Lesotho	•	•	•	•	•	•	•	•		•	•	•														
Kenya	•	•						•		•	•	•														
Guinea-Bissau										•	•	•														
Guinea		•					•		•	•																
Ghana	•	•	•	•		•		•	•	•	•															
Gambia	•	•	•	•	•	•	•	•	•	•	•	•														
Gabon		•	•					•		•	•														•	
Egypt	•	•	•	•						•				•			•	•			•		•		•	
Djibouti								•		•																
Dem. Rep. of the Congo	•	•	•	•		•			•	•																
Côte d'Ivoire		•	•	•			•		•	•		•										•				
Congo								•	•	•																
Chad								•		•																
Central African Republic	•	•	•			•		•		•	•															
Cabo Verde	•	•	•	•	•	•		•		•															•	
Cameroon	•	•	•						•	•		•														
Burundi	•	•		•	•				•	•											•					
Burkina Faso	•	•	•	•					•	•																
Botswana	•	•	•																							
Benin										•																
Angola	•							•	•	•		•													•	

Source: Developed by UNCTAD, based on country schedules of commitments, http://i-tip.wto.org/services/Search.aspx (accessed 5 April 2015).

services and financial services (20 countries each). The least frequently inscribed sector is other services not included elsewhere (4 countries), followed by distribution services (6 countries) and health-related and social services (7 countries). With regard to MFN exemptions, the sector figuring most frequently is transport services, with 15 countries having inscribed it in their list of exemptions, and less prominently financial services, in 7 countries.

Despite the high degree of heterogeneity, some common policy observations can be derived from the study of these schedules. First, the tourism and travel sectors have a clear prominence for liberalization in almost all of the 42 African schedules of commitments, especially in modes 1 and 2. For example, this would correspond to activities such as online bookings and tourism agencies for the former, and tourist travel, tour operators, and the hospitality and transport industries, for the latter. This is no different from other world regions where the same type of liberalization has been deep and has resulted in a niching of tourism services, such as medical tourism in Hungary or wedding tourism in the Caribbean. Over the past decade, strong growth has characterized the African services sector, particularly tourism, and the schedules show some alignment with the aforementioned regional and national policies.

A second commonality relates to a disconnect between the schedules of commitments of some African members and the sectors they have been pushing forward at the national level, especially under modes 1 and 2. For example, Kenya and more recently Senegal, have become major exporters of business process outsourcing services (Stephenson, 2012), but business services do not figure prominently in their schedule of commitments. Lastly, Burkina Faso is known as a leading exporter of cultural services which contributes 2 per cent of its GDP (African Union, 2014a, 2014 b). However, its schedule omits recreational, cultural and sporting services. In all these cases, these sectors present opportunities that could lead to job creation, economic growth and development, yet there is a disconnect between national prioritization and the global dimension.

This disconnect has been subject to heavy criticism in the past and has been mainly attributed to the fact that some countries negotiated unprepared for the level of complexity of GATS and indeed gave away more than they should have at the time. This led to proposals by African countries to make a sober assessment of trade in services and the feasibility of offers being requested (WTO, 2002). This has also been compounded by criticism about whether the GATS architecture is development friendly and whether African countries have been able to take advantage of the special and differential treatment provisions contained therein (Mattoo and Subramanian, 2003; Kessie and Apea, 2004).

The validity of such criticism for African member States underpins the importance of policy consistency and alignment at three policymaking levels: the national level, the regional and pan-African level, and the global level. This is particularly relevant when a sovereign State may be considering policy decisions domestically to support the development of a sector or infant industry. Sectors that may be deemed to enjoy protection through sectoral or industrial policies or are being spearheaded as national or regional champions could give rise to inconsistencies with existing GATS obligations.

A third commonality relates to what African countries consider priority carve-outs of their GATS schedules. In 10 of the 15 MFN exemptions that pertain to transport services shown in table 11, mention is made of cabotage, liner and shipping rights that could be granted in the future to trade partners either in the context of bilateral or multilateral agreements. It appears as a paradox that two landlocked countries (Mali and the Niger) and another eight coastal countries with virtually non-existent maritime industries would hold such exemptions.

These type of carve-outs[11] may be considered negotiating cards to be traded in the future against market access in other sectors, given the political economy of multilateral trade rounds. But beyond the political economy of cross-sectoral negotiations, there are important gains that African countries could reap from maritime transport liberalization, albeit partial through regional trade agreements, especially as the major shipping lines on the continent are mostly serviced by a select number of foreign liners from developed countries. These liners are known to operate in an oligopolistic manner, contributing to the already high costs of shipping commodities from Africa, and have a bearing on the export earnings of African producers (Anderson and Yao, 2001). In particular, these liners accrue large earnings, as they form part of global value chains in two ways: they are the backbone of the maritime transport services value chains, and they in themselves form part of all value chains of merchandise trade goods that are shipped. Hence, developing the sector in Africa constitutes an important opportunity to participate in both. In most schedules with this type of carve-out, countries justifications for these exemptions include the promotion of their international trade, regional integration and/or the development of an infant industry, for example a national maritime fleet.

Another priority exemption is financial services in a total of 7 of the 17 schedules featuring MFN exemptions. These mostly pertain to existing regional integration arrangements, such as the West African Economic and Monetary Union and the CFA franc zone in the case of Côte d'Ivoire; ECOWAS and the West African Economic and Monetary Union in the case of Senegal; and South Africa and Swaziland in the case of the Common Monetary Area of the rand. Mauritius, for example, conditions access to modes 1 and 3 of commercial banking on the basis of reciprocity. Here, regional integration again appears as a major priority in the carve-outs and is being aligned with global commitments.

Because services trade is covered through horizontal, sectoral and modal delivery in GATS, horizontal limitations — even if not reflected in the sectoral part of the schedules — can have a bearing on the type of access to a services market in a given country. It is important to remember that the schedule should be read and interpreted as a whole document and that the level of protection afforded to a particular sector can only be ascertained by what has been inscribed in the horizontal, sector and MFN exemptions sections of a country schedule.

Table 12 summarizes some of the key highlights of the horizontal commitments that have a bearing on investment and employment across the services sectors in 20 of the 42 African schedules. There are a total of 112 commitments comprising 69 market access limitations and 43 national treatment limitations. Almost all focus on services delivery through mode 3 (43 commitments) and mode 4 (63 commitments). There are only three market access limitations for modes 1 and 2 each in the schedules of Botswana, Morocco and Tunisia. These relate mainly to issues of capital transfer, requiring the approval of the central bank or are linked to exchange controls regulations prevailing in these three countries.

In terms of the scope and coverage of these limitations, there are considerable variations of how commitments are phrased. However, most can be grouped as follows: admission, authorization, licensing and/or notification requirements of foreign services firms seeking to operate in a given market; limitations on the form, amount and/or control of FDI; limitations on the participation in mergers and acquisitions (M&A) and/or privatizations processes; limitations on leasing or purchasing real estate; limitation on subsidies, tax holidays, transfers or related preferential treatment; establishment, approval, registration and/or residency requirements; qualification, skills or employment requirements; limitations on the category and/or functions of foreign employees; limitations on the duration of stay of foreign employees; and economic and/or social needs or labour market tests.

Table 12. Horizontal measures affecting investment and employment in services of African schedules of the General Agreement on Trade in Services

Country	Admission/ authorization/ licensing or notification requirements	Limitations on form/ amount or control of FDI	Limitations to participating in M&As/ privatization	Limitations on the lease/ purchase of real estate	Limitations on subsidies/tax write-offs/transfers/preferential treatment	Establishment approval/ registration or residency requirements	Qualification/ skills or employment requirements	Limitations on the category/ function of employees	Limitations on the duration of stay[a]	Economic needs/ social benefit or labour market tests
Botswana	MA 3, NT 3	NT 3	NT 3		MA 1, 2	MA 4, NT 4	MA 4, NT 4	MA 4		MA 4
Burundi		MA 3					MA 4	MA 4, NT 4		
Cameroon	MA 3							MA 4		MA 3
Cabo Verde				MA 3, 4					MA 4	NT 3
Dem. Rep. of the Congo	MA 3, NT 3			MA 3, NT 3			MA 4, NT 4	MA 4, NT 4	MA 4, NT 4	
Egypt				NT 3			MA 4	MA 4		
Gambia	MA 3	MA 3				MA 3, MA*4		MA* 4		MA* 4
Ghana		MA 3						NT 4		
Kenya		MA 3				MA 4	NT 4	NT 4		NT 4
Lesotho		MA 3					NT 4	NT 4		NT 4
Malawi					NT 3	MA 4		MA* 4		
Mauritius		MA* 3		MA* 3	MA* 3	MA* 3		NT 4		
Morocco		MA 3			MA 1, 2, 4	MA 4	MA 4	MA 4	MA 4	
Namibia		MA 3				MA 4	MA 4	MA 4		
Nigeria		MA 3		MA 3						
Sierra Leone		MA 3		MA 3			MA 4	MA 4		MA 4
South Africa					NT 3		NT 4	MA* 4	MA* 4	
Tunisia	MA & NT 3, 4	NT 3, 4		MA & NT 3, 4	MA 1, 2	NT 3, 4	MA 4	MA 4		
Zambia							MA 4	MA* 4		MA 4
Zimbabwe	MA 3	MA 3			NT 3			MA 4		MA 4

Source: Developed by UNCTAD based on country schedules of commitments, http://i-tip.wto.org/services/Search.aspx (accessed 5 April 2015).

Note: a Refers to expressly stated limitations on the number of years, months or days.

Modes of supply: 1 = cross-border trade, 2 = consumption abroad, 3 = commercial presence, 4 = presence of natural persons.

Abbreviations: MA, market access column; NT, national treatment column; MA*, limitations inscribed in market access column also apply to national treatment.

The most frequently represented restrictions are those that have to do with limitations pertaining to the category and/or function of foreign employees (mode 4), followed by limitations on the form, amount or control of FDI (mode 3). This is no different from what developed countries such as those in the OECD region tend to restrict more prominently. Indeed, certain modes of delivery may influence investment and employment considerations in the host economy. For example, mode 3, which relates to commercial presence of foreign services providers, may be a conduit for more or less FDI if limitations under this mode inscribed in a schedule require that commercial presence be in a particular form, for example, a subsidiary of a foreign company as opposed to a branch. For instance, in the case of commercial banks, the type of commercial presence can be shaped by the limitations inscribed in the market access and national treatment columns of the schedules, and hence influence the type of FDI coming into the banking sector (Páez, 2008a, 2011).

Because the limitations inscribed in the schedules under mode 4 deal with domestic regulation that governs the behaviour of foreign service providers, they will have a bearing on the hiring practices of such providers. Many of the schedules contain economic and social needs tests and training requirements pertaining to the hiring of local staff. These are typical industrial policy provisions that are applied when some form of beneficiation or crowding in is desired in a given sector.

Potential gains from services trade through the General Agreement on Trade in Services are within reach.

After an analysis of the schedules of commitments it is important to consider how African member States could enhance the potential benefits derived from GATS services trade.[12] An important aspect of services trade that has been largely out of bounds for African countries relates to labour mobility, which is not covered in GATS, except for mode 4, which covers the temporary movement of persons. This may hold the greatest potential for developing countries, if flexibility is applied to the Agreement (Kessie, 2000; Mattoo and Subramanian, 2003; Mavroidis, 2004).

However, in order for this promise to materialize, developed country members of WTO would need to offer adequate market access to developing countries' service providers under mode 4. If exclusively targeted at Africa, they would have to be able to discriminate between developing countries, which in the past has been challenged in WTO. In Africa, this is all the more important, as its youth is expected to double by 2025. Given these trends and current jobless growth (UNCTAD, 2013b), it is critical that efforts be focused on generating employment, especially for young people.

African countries have been cautious about opening up mode 4, but have made far-reaching commitments at the regional level, with important implications for the continent's population. These efforts need to be accompanied by similar developments at the global level. Therefore, it will be important to support the recent GATS waiver tabled by Uganda on behalf of the least developed countries (LDCs). If properly instrumentalized, the waiver could deliver additional gains for 34 African LDCs, as described in box 4. Advocacy and a rigorous monitoring and evaluation and accountability framework will be necessary if the waiver is to have an impact.

Beyond the waiver, African countries should continue using their influence as a group to articulate common positions in WTO that reflect more clearly the pressing needs of enhanced services trade at the national and regional levels. This has been done in the past for services and other sectors, with some notable success.[13] For services trade, African countries could call for greater efforts towards a more relaxed interpretation of GATS rules pertaining to the interpretation of article V, which allows for the creation of regional trade agreements in violation of the MFN principle, especially since existing regional integration programmes have components that allow differing speeds to open up sectors according to a country's level of development. This is also particularly important for the future of pan-African initiatives such as the tripartite and the CFTA, which envisage the gradual incorporation of services in their liberalization programmes.

Box 4. The General Agreement of Trade in Services waiver for least developed countries: Progress towards its operationalization

During the eighth WTO ministerial conference in 2011, a waiver was adopted that allows for exceptions from the MFN provision in GATS article II — a provision that requires WTO members to provide non-discriminatory treatment to all their trading partners. The waiver allows members to provide preferential treatment to services and services suppliers of LDCs with respect to market access and other measures. While preferential treatment concerning market access is allowed automatically under the waiver, preferential treatment with regard to non-market access provisions is subject to approval by the Council for Trade in Services. The waiver applies to all LDCs, including those that are not members of WTO. This makes the waiver critical to Africa, as 34 of the 48 LDCs are African; it also presents an opportunity for an early harvest for African LDCs that are not members.

Since no members have made use of the waiver to date, a decision to initiate a process to operationalize the waiver was adopted during the ninth WTO ministerial conference in 2013. Following that decision, a collective request identifying the sectors and modes of supply of most interest to LDCs was submitted by the LDC group in July 2014. The decision also established that this submission should be followed by a high-level meeting six months later, in which members are expected to indicate sectors and modes of supply where they intend to provide preferential treatment to LDCs.

Box 4 (continued)

The LDC group submission calls for members to waive market access and national treatment restrictions through both horizontal and sector-specific measures. With regard to the former, the submission suggests that restrictions should be waived through, inter alia, the creation of special temporary entry visa subcategories to allocate quotas for LDC service suppliers and waiving of economic needs and labour market tests. The submission also urges members to waive restrictions on certain sectors, including tourism, banking, transport, ICT and business process outsourcing services, as well as certain restrictions relating to visas and permits, the recognition of qualifications of LDC professionals and accreditation of LDC institutions.

The services waiver offers opportunities to enhance growth and development by promoting the growth of services sectors in LDCs (Stephenson and Pfister, 2013). For instance, access to developed markets for African workers could enhance African LDCs' services exports and would provide an avenue for diaspora and mobile workers to obtain short-term gainful employment that would boost remittances to LDC economies. This would, however, require not only market access but also the recognition of African qualifications (Stern and Ward, 2013). Indeed, most trade barriers are not market access restrictions but rather qualitative barriers such as domestic regulations (Manrique Carpio and Comas Mir, 2014). As the major obstacle is often regulation, the waiver has the potential to improve prospects for LDC services suppliers. Examples of such preferences are facilitated licensing procedures and lower application fees for LDC services suppliers and the recognition of qualifications based on practical experience for LDC professionals (Schloemann, 2012).

African countries need to be mindful of their opportunities and their preferred preferential treatment to achieve a meaningful result from forthcoming negotiations. It will be particularly important for African LDCs to identify priority sectors where quotas for professionals and service providers would be desirable, specify the adequate size of the quotas and clearly indicate how practical experience comparable to a formal qualification should be defined in order to best serve the interests of LDCs.

Sources: Based on WTO, 2011, 2013, 2014.

E. BRIDGING THE DISCONNECT OF AFRICAN SERVICES POLICIES: TOWARDS A COHERENT STRATEGY FOR ENHANCED SERVICES TRADE

Africa has made important strides towards the regulation and promotion of its services sector. The mapping exercise of the African services policies at the national, regional and global levels carried out in this chapter revealed that there are multiple layers of policy at the national, regional and pan-African, and global levels that attempt to regulate and promote the services sector in Africa. However, these multiple layers of regulation appear disjointed and unrelated across existing national, regional and global frameworks. This disarticulation makes it difficult for Africa to make the most of the opportunities of enhancing services trade for growth and development.

As discussed previously, a disconnect can be observed at three levels:

a) At the national level where most countries reviewed during the mapping exercise portrayed insufficient linkage in their national strategy documents with the services trade agendas they are promoting at the regional and global levels;

b) At the regional level, where some of the major regional protocols emulate the GATS language on services trade, but fail to articulate a coordinated and permanent consultation mechanism that allows them to put forward their regional priorities and concerns at both the national and multilateral levels;

c) At the global level where from the supply side, the African country schedules fail to reflect certain priority sectors that countries and regions could be championing more adequately, and where from the demand side, African countries have been shy of tabling their national and regional needs more effectively in the WTO services agenda.

Without well-articulated, consistent services policies, it will be difficult to ascertain the impact of any policy intervention or calibration, let alone maximize its contribution in harnessing the services sector for economic development. If African countries are to capture the gains of adequate policy formulation, it is necessary to introduce greater consistency and coherence into the policy processes at the three levels.

Given the need for enhanced policy articulation, this section sketches out a regional strategy to address the policy disconnect of African services policy. It does so by proposing policy processes that build on the national, regional and global dimensions of policymaking and by suggesting the use of existing regional mechanisms at the pan-African level that could take the lead in coordinating and articulating policy directives that ensure consistency and coherence at the three policymaking levels.

Addressing the disconnect at the national level: Mainstreaming services trade policy into national development plans

Most African countries have a national development plan, and most of the countries studied here were found to mention services in that document. However, the degree to which services trade is linked to development objectives and forms part of that process varies considerably from country to country.

Strategy documents such as national development plans should clearly indicate how services trade forms part of a greater development agenda. African policymakers formulating these documents need to envision the ways in which the services sector could be a conduit for their development outcomes such as inclusive growth, employment and poverty reduction. It is critical to link this vision to existing regional integration plans and visions that exist at the regional economic community level, as well as the pan-African level.

Consequently, to mainstream services trade policy effectively, a process must be implemented. This process requires that a policy formulation exercise be informed by country-wide consultations to determine what is being prioritized, who will receive the delegated authority of the services trade mandate and who are the major stakeholders. Consultations should constitute an integral part of the policy process from the outset, as they are critical to help ensure that a greater sense of national ownership and understanding of the policy outcome is developed.

For the subsequent implementation of the strategy set out for services trade, the same language needs then to be mirrored at lower policy levels. In other words, policy documents that turn the vision into action should be elaborated, such as a trade policy and also sectoral policies, programmes and regulation. At this level, policymakers involved in formulating trade policy will need to clearly articulate how services trade forms part of the process of upgrading and moving up global value chains from the lower to the higher end of productive activities. This also needs to properly reflect the role services will play in the structural transformation of the economy, if it is ultimately deemed to have a meaningful contribution and role to play in that process. The same exercise must be consistently undertaken for any given services sector that a country may wish to champion or prioritize, and both the trade policy and sectoral policy documents that are developed must be consistent with each other.

A greater degree of specificity and detail will be required at this level, so that services trade may be adequately mainstreamed into the economy. Once again, consistent linkage to existing regional integration programmes and policies that target services should also be adequately reflected, and institutional channels for a continuous dialogue between the national and the regional spheres, established. Equally important is the development of links to the global level, in the context of the WTO services trade negotiations, and how the country makes use of that platform to position its services trade needs.

Lastly, national policy processes at any level should cater for monitoring and evaluation frameworks that allow for a continuous assessment of the progress being made during implementation. This will include the formulation of clearly defined targets, activities, outputs, outcomes and impact that are clearly formulated and time bound. Only by ensuring that a proper monitoring and evaluation and accountability framework is in place can policy outcomes and impact be closely linked to activities and outputs and corrective action be taken if targets are not being met.

Addressing the disconnect at the regional level: Continuous consultation and coordination through a pan-African mechanism

At the regional level, greater coherence may be achieved if a pan-African mechanism is established to allow for the continuous consultation and coordination of a regional agenda and concerns relating to services trade that arise within the regional economic communities and the African Union. In essence, it would allow for the cross-fertilization of services trade priorities stemming from the consultations in regional economic communities, among them and in the African Union, which could then be relayed to the national and multilateral levels through the decision-making process of the African Union. To date, most of the services trade agenda at the regional economic community level has been influenced by the GATS negotiations, from a top-down approach. Having such a mechanism in place would also allow for a more institutionalized and strengthened bottom-up influencing process of what transpires in the negotiations of the Africa Group based in Geneva (WTO), Brussels (European Union economic partnership agreements) and the United States of America (the African Growth and Opportunity Act).

Such a mechanism could be vested in the High-Level African Trade Committee, which forms part of the governance structure of the CFTA and has been mandated to observe progress made in trade liberalization by the African Union Heads of State and Government. This mechanism has already been put into action for trade facilitation, in the context of the implementation of the Agreement on Trade Facilitation according to the decision taken at the Bali Ministerial (African Union, 2014c). This is a clear example of how the alignment of the WTO negotiations on trade facilitation with existing priorities of trade facilitation under the CFTA could be pursued for services trade.

Addressing the disconnect at the global level: Making use of existing mechanisms of the World Trade Organization and instrumentalizing the services waiver

At the global level, African countries individually and collectively should ensure that their national and regional priorities are better taken into account and adequately reflected in the global services agenda in order to move from the multi-layered status quo to an articulated strategy at the three levels on trade in services.

From a country and regional perspective, policymakers need to reflect carefully about what constitutes their interests in services trade from both the demand side as well as the supply side of negotiations. As discussed earlier, the supply side does not currently reflect the needs of some of the sectors being championed by African member States at the national and regional levels. A major challenge will be how to achieve greater policy space, given that GATS does not allow for backtracking on previous commitments.

In short, African countries have three options:

a) To make a case for greater flexibility in the interpretation of GATS rules, in order to afford them sufficient policy space to continue championing those sectors;

b) To make sure that for those sectors that have not yet been committed and represent a national or regional priority, analytical work is conducted to develop commitments that reflect such priorities and that they can be negotiated in future trade rounds in WTO;

c) To prioritize which sectors may be best suited to benefit from a regional negotiating strategy within the Africa Group or other subgroupings in the context of the WTO negotiations process, as is currently being done with the GATS waiver.

A relevant question arises at this point. How do African countries make a compelling case for affording sufficient policy space for a strategic sector such as financial services, where greater financial inclusion is a national priority? The next chapter discusses the international regulatory and supervisory context of reconciling financial services innovations, cross-border banking and financial inclusion with an increasingly liberalized trade environment.

CHAPTER **4**

UNLOCKING FINANCIAL SERVICES POTENTIAL IN AFRICA THROUGH CROSS-BORDER BANKING

A. INTRODUCTION

A well-functioning financial system is critical to Africa's long-term growth. The financial sector can promote economic growth, stimulate investment and contribute to poverty reduction (Demirguc-Kunt, 2006; Fry, 1995). This chapter discusses the importance of financial inclusion in the context of financial sector development, the regulatory dimensions of financial services trade in the context of growing banking internationalization in Africa, and the importance of striking a balance between domestic development priorities and policy space in relation to liberalization commitments, rising competition and foreign entry. The chapter concludes with policy recommendations on how countries can approach the regulatory dilemma they often face, between greater financial inclusion on the one hand and liberalization on the other.

B. FINANCIAL SECTOR DEVELOPMENT IN AFRICA: DEPTH AND ACCESS ISSUES

Financial depth

A useful starting point for an analysis of the role of financial services in economic development in Africa is to consider its contribution to GDP. Despite the empirical challenges of estimating the contribution of financial services to the economy, a number of observations may be drawn from the data. Table 13 shows that financial depth as measured by M2 as a share of GDP[14] is much lower in Africa than most other developing regions. In comparative terms, the formal financial sector in Africa performed more poorly during the period 2009–2012, as monetary resources mobilized by the sector was 42.1 per cent on average, compared with 76.5 per cent in other developing countries and the world average of 72.3 per cent.

Table 13 shows that there is a wide range of variation in private credit to GDP across Africa according to export orientation (classification). In terms of export-orientated manufactures (41.2 per cent) and services (38.1 per cent), exporters reported much higher private credit to GDP ratios than fuel (12.2 per cent) and ores/metals (16.7 per cent) exporters. Across the continent, private credit-to-GDP ratios range from 4.5 per cent in the Democratic Republic of the Congo and Chad to 90.7 per cent in Mauritius.

While there has been improvement in all three indicators from 2000 to 2013 and the average M2 ratio to GDP has increased from 35 per cent to 42 per cent (table

Table 13. Financial depth indicators

Exports specialization	Liquid liabilities (M3) as percentage of GDP		Money and quasi money (M2) as percentage of GDP		Bank deposits to GDP (percentage)		Domestic credit to private sector by banks (percentag of GDP)	
	2001–2004	2009–2012	2001–2004	2009–2012	2001–2004	2009–2011	2001–2004	2009–2012
Fuel	*44.6*	*46.4*	*22.5*	*33.4*	*13.5*	*22.8*	*8.2*	*12.2*
Algeria	44.6	46.4	57.9	63.1	38.8	44.6	10.6	14.9
Angola	..	..	18.5	37.6	11.1	29.3	4.5	20.9
Chad	..	..	11.3	11.6	4.0	6.1	4.0	4.6
Congo	..	..	12.5	25.8	6.7	14.7	3.6	7.2
Equatorial Guinea	..	..	8.1	17.2	4.7	10.2	3.5	8.8
Gabon	..	..	16.3	20.3	12.8	16.1	12.2	9.6
Libya	..	..	41.3	74.6	21.6	39.1	16.3	12.6
Nigeria	..	..	21.7	26.5	15.1	32.2	14.1	19.5
South Sudan	..	..	..	..			..	..
Sudan	..	..	14.9	24.1	6.9	13.4	5.3	11.8
Food and agriculture	*21.5*	*32.4*	*20.3*	*32.1*	*9.9*	*18.7*	*6.7*	*14.5*
Côte d'Ivoire	24.9	34.5	24.9	34.5	13.3	21.6	14.5	16.6
Guinea-Bissau	20.2	30.3	20.2	30.3	5.3	12.7	1.2	8.8
Malawi	19.4	..	15.9	31.3	11.1	21.9	4.5	17.9
Somalia	..	..	..	..	..	..	..	..
Ores and metal	*28.2*	*25.5*	*22.0*	*28.4*	*14.7*	*22.3*	*9.7*	*16.7*
Botswana	..	..	44.9	46.5	24.5	44.0	19.4	28.4
Democratic Rep. of the Congo	..	..	3.5	10.2	2.4	..	0.7	4.5
Guinea	..	..	15.3	33.3	..	17.3	3.7	6.2
Mauritania	..	..	..	33.6	15.7	19.5	..	28.0
Mali	28.2	29.1	28.2	29.1	..	21.7	18.6	19.3
Zambia	..	16.2	18.3	18.8	16.1	9.2	6.1	10.3
Manufactured goods	*54.0*	*67.5*	*41.5*	*52.1*	*35.9*	*42.1*	*32.8*	*41.2*
Tunisia	54.0	67.5	51.6	65.3	45.9	50.7	55.2	67.3
Lesotho	..	..	31.3	38.8	25.9	33.5	10.3	15.1
Services	*48.0*	*26.2*	*42.4*	*60.5*	*32.5*	*46.4*	*20.0*	*38.1*
Cabo Verde	..	..	71.1	79.5	58.9	72.5	33.0	61.8
Comoros	14.1	26.2	26.1	36.6	13.4	23.0	7.4	18.6
Djibouti	..	..	65.4	84.8	51.8	71.7	23.6	29.7
Ethiopia	43.8	..	42.9	..	32.3	..	17.4	..
Gambia	..	..	28.7	50.8	39.1	35.1	9.6	15.3
Liberia	..	..	13.1	35.4	7.2	32.0	4.3	14.6
Mauritius	86.1	..	90.2	99.8	15.2	16.4	65.6	90.7

Table 13 (contd.)

Exports specialization	Liquid liabilities (M3) as percentage of GDP		Money and quasi money (M2) as percentage of GDP		Bank deposits to GDP (percentage)		Domestic credit to private sector by banks (percentag of GDP)	
	2001–2004	2009–2012	2001–2004	2009–2012	2001–2004	2009–2011	2001–2004	2009–2012
Rwanda	..	..	17.4	..	75.5	90.8	10.2	..
Sao Tome and Principe	..	..	26.5	36.6	13.0	..	8.8	35.9
Seychelles	90.2	53.5	102.7	57.0	18.9	29.6	21.9	22.2
Madagascar	..	..	23.7	24.1	89.2	54.2	8.8	11.3
Mixed exporters	*31.6*	*33.6*	*39.3*	*44.1*	*24.6*	*32.3*	*21.8*	*25.9*
Benin	26.4	38.9	26.4	38.9	16.1	26.9	12.7	23.6
Burkina Faso	21.5	28.3	21.5	28.3	13.4	21.1	13.5	18.7
Burundi	16.2	20.5	21.0	24.9	18.6	18.6	18.3	16.9
Cameroon	..	..	15.7	20.8	12.3	17.4	9.2	13.1
Central African Republic	..	..	15.3	17.8	3.8	8.1	6.3	9.6
Egypt	..	..	91.2	78.4	72.6	65.5	54.4	32.4
Eritrea	..	..	143.8	119.8	..	..	26.8	14.8
Ghana	..	..	32.3	29.7	18.0	21.0	12.3	14.8
Kenya	39.5	..	37.9	39.6	31.9	40.0	25.7	28.0
Morocco	..	..	77.5	111.1	61.4	84.7	43.1	69.6
Mozambique	..	..	27.2	39.0	21.3	32.4	11.6	23.5
Namibia	..	..	36.6	61.8	37.1	58.1	43.6	48.9
Niger	11.3	20.7	11.3	20.7	6.6	11.1	5.3	13.1
Senegal	29.4	39.2	29.4	39.2	20.7	28.8	19.1	27.2
Sierra Leone	..	..	13.9	21.3	..	18.0	2.4	7.6
South Africa	41.4	42.9	61.7	77.8	50.6	60.7	65.8	72.7
Swaziland	..	..	20.2	29.1	18.1	27.0	13.6	23.6
Togo	26.0	44.7	26.0	44.7	18.1	31.7	15.2	25.3
Uganda	..	..	18.0	25.2	12.8	16.5	7.6	15.8
United Republic of Tanzania	19.7	..	22.2	33.2	15.6	25.2	6.7	16.5
Zimbabwe	84.6	..	75.4	..	17.9	..	45.3	..
World	*48.6*	*46.5*	*59.0*	*72.3*	*44.0*	*55.8*	*39.6*	*55.2*
Africa total	*37.1*	*37.0*	*35.1*	*42.1*	*24.2*	*31.8*	*17.2*	*23.6*
East Asia and Pacific	*47.3*	*52.8*	*73.3*	*88.7*	*60.3*	*68.6*	*49.9*	*64.1*
Latin America and Caribbean	*35.8*	*39.7*	*55.2*	*61.2*	*45.0*	*50.7*	*38.5*	*45.4*
South Asia	*43.8*	*52.9*	*48.6*	*56.1*	*38.8*	*46.2*	*24.7*	*36.9*
Other developing countries	*55.3*	*48.3*	*71.6*	*76.5*	*44.0*	*66.5*	*35.8*	*45.6*

Source: UNCTAD secretariat calculations, based on data from the *World Development Indicators* (World Bank, 2014) and the *Global Finance Development* database, February 2015.

13), Africa's financial sector remains shallow in comparison with other developing regions. Even during the global financial crisis of 2008–2009, credit to the private sector in relation to GDP increased on average, although by less than deposits. From 2001 to 2004 and 2009 to 2012, the credit-to-GDP ratio also increased — from 17.2 to 23.6 per cent — but this did not necessarily translate into significant financial deepening.

The financial sector is highly heterogeneous, given the economic size of a country or depth of banking markets (table 13). South Africa, Mauritius, Morocco and Nigeria generally report the highest continental levels of financial development. Even some countries with comparatively small populations such as the Seychelles have relatively large offshore financial services sectors. This heterogeneity may be one of the main obstacles to the development of an integrated framework for continental cross-border supervision.

Financial access

The United Nations defines the goals of financial inclusion as follows:

a) Access at a reasonable cost for all households to a full range of financial services, including savings or deposit services, payment and transfer services, credit and insurance;

b) Sound and safe institutions governed by clear regulation and industry performance standards;

c) Financial and institutional sustainability, to ensure continuity and certainty of investment;

d) Competition, to ensure choice and affordability for clients (United Nations Capital Development Fund, 2006).

In 2011, roughly 21.5 per cent of Africa's population had access to formal financial services, compared with 54.9 per cent in East Asia and the Pacific, 31.3 per cent in South Asia and 42.7 per cent in other developing countries (see figure 6). The unbanked are largely women (only 20 per cent had access to formal financial services), the rural population and the urban poor (Demirguc-Kunt and Klapper, 2012).

Within Africa, there is a large variation in formal account ownership, ranging from 80 per cent in Mauritius to 1.5 per cent in the Niger (see table 14). Less than 5 per cent of adults have an account at a formal financial institution in the Niger, the Central African Republic, the Democratic Republic of the Congo and Guinea.

Figure 6. Adults holding an account at a formal financial institution, by rural-urban designation, 2011 (Percentage)

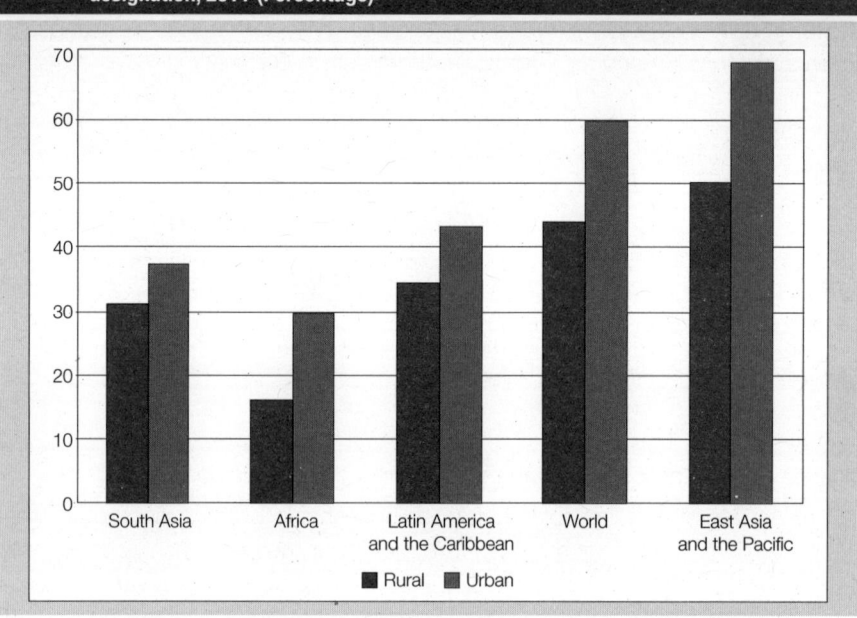

Source: UNCTAD secretariat calculations, based on data from Demirguc-Kunt and Klapper, 2012.

Some countries such as Egypt, which have relatively well-developed financial sectors, have well below the continental average levels of access to formal financial services, particularly in rural areas. If export orientation is used as the base criterion, the services (28.5 per cent) exporters' category is above the continental average for formal financial account penetration (see table 14).

A variety of obstacles to financial inclusion have been reported, such as the lack of demand for financial services due to limited disposable income as a main reason for not having a bank account. Also, financial exclusion caused by physical, economic, and administrative barriers such as cost, travel distance, bureaucracy and a lack of trust in the banking system play a role. Greater financial inclusion will require development strategies that make financial services available to the aforementioned groups and SMEs. Since the 1980s, financial sector development strategies have mainly focused on achieving stability and efficiency, and increasing the availability of finance to Government and large firms.

Table 14. Financial access indicators

Exports specialization	Depositors with commercial banks (per 1,000 adults)		Borrowers from commercial banks (per 1,000 adults)		Commercial bank branches (per 100,000 adults)		Account-holders at a formal financial institution aged 15+ (percentage)		Automated teller machines (per 100,000 adults)		Mobile phones used to pay bills by users aged 15+ (percentage)	
	2001–2004	2009–2012	2001–2004	2009–2012	2001–2004	2009–2012	2001–2004	2009–2011	2001–2004	2009–2012	2001–2004	2009–2011
Fuel	*226.6*	*292.0*	*31.1*	*38.0*	*3.3*	*5.3*	..	*20.9*	*0.9*	*6.3*	..	*5.4*
Algeria	330.8	352.7	25.2	37.3	4.6	5.0	..	33.3	1.2	5.7	..	9.7
Angola	..	87.1	..	..	2.2	9.2	..	39.2	1.0	14.3	..	13.6
Chad	5.7	18.5	0.4	2.6	0.4	0.6	..	9.0	0.0	0.4	..	2.8
Congo	14.7	67.4	..	24.1	0.7	2.4	..	9.0	0.5	2.2	..	1.6
Equatorial Guinea	100.2	196.6	2.8	12.4	3.2	4.7	..	..	0.0	5.6	..	..
Gabon	..	174.5	2.0	28.5	2.4	5.6	..	18.9	0.6	10.0	..	4.9
Libya	681.4	755.3	125.4	152.0	9.2	11.5	..	..	3.6	3.7	..	..
Nigeria	..	517.2	..	29.3	4.7	6.3	..	29.7	..	11.4	..	1.4
South Sudan	..	..	..	..	..	..	..	..	..	..	..	..
Sudan	..	..	..	..	2.5	2.7	..	6.9	0.0	3.2	..	4.0
Food and agriculture	*41.3*	*133.6*	..	*16.5*	*0.8*	*2.8*	..	*23.8*	*0.7*	*3.1*	..	*13.5*
Côte d'Ivoire	73.5	168.7	..	..	1.3	4.0	..	..	..	4.3	..	..
Guinea-Bissau	9.0	61.0	..	..	0.1	2.1	..	..	..	1.7	..	..
Malawi	..	176.3	..	16.5	1.0	2.4	..	16.5	0.7	3.4	..	0.8
Somalia	..	..	..	..	..	..	..	31.0	..	..	..	26.2
Ores and metal	*101.0*	*164.8*	*47.2*	*72.1*	*3.1*	*3.9*	..	*14.1*	*7.7*	*10.0*	..	*2.3*
Botswana	337.1	500.1	139.9	195.3	6.5	8.6	..	30.3	14.6	27.3	..	2.2
Democratic Rep. of the Congo	0.5	17.1	0.0	1.7	0.5	0.6	..	3.7	..	0.4	..	0.1
Guinea	..	..	..	..	..	1.2	..	3.7	..	..	..	1.1
Mauritania	..	54.9	..	43.0	..	4.4	..	8.2	..	..	..	0.3
Mali	53.4	112.7	..	..	2.4	3.7	..	17.5	..	3.1	..	7.5
Zambia	13.1	27.5	1.5	18.7	3.1	4.2	..	21.4	0.9	7.3	..	2.4
Manufactured goods	*233.2*	*574.5*	*41.1*	*122.1*	*7.3*	*9.9*	..	*25.3*	*5.7*	*14.3*	..	*2.3*
Tunisia	..	732.6	75.3	165.3	12.0	16.6	..	32.2	8.5	20.8	..	0.0
Lesotho	233.2	297.3	6.8	42.9	2.6	3.2	..	18.5	2.9	7.8	..	4.6
Services	*323.0*	*396.5*	*30.2*	*32.6*	*4.4*	*10.6*	..	*28.5*	*5.4*	*13.1*	..	*1.9*
Cabo Verde	890.2	1437.2	82.6	122.0	..	29.8	..	..	..	42.0	..	..
Comoros	71.5	75.1	7.7	7.0	0.6	1.4	..	21.7	0.6	4.9	..	0.3
Djibouti	..	78.3	..	17.9	2.0	4.7	..	12.3	0.8	3.2	..	2.8
Ethiopia	..	110.4	..	1.8	0.8	1.9	..	..	0.0	0.3	..	..
Gambia	..	..	..	..	4.3	8.8	..	..	..	..	..	..
Liberia	..	..	..	..	..	3.5	..	18.8	..	1.4	..	5.2
Mauritius	..	..	..	..	18.0	21.0	..	80.1	30.7	41.1	..	0.0

Table 14 (contd.)

Exports specialization	Depositors with commercial banks (per 1,000 adults)		Borrowers from commercial banks (per 1,000 adults)		Commercial bank branches (per 100,000 adults)		Account-holders at a formal financial institution aged 15+ (percentage)		Automated teller machines (per 100,000 adults)		Mobile phones used to pay bills by users aged 15+ (percentage)	
	2001–2004	2009–2012	2001–2004	2009–2012	2001–2004	2009–2012	2001–2004	2009–2011	2001–2004	2009–2012	2001–2004	2009–2011
Rwanda	7.4	214.0	0.4	6.9	0.4	5.7	..	32.8	0.0	2.4	..	1.8
Sao Tome and Principe	..	463.7	..	..	..	22.1	..		0.0	9.4	..	1.1
Seychelles	275.0	780.0	76.1	133.6	42.0	46.8	..		34.0	46.4	..	..
Madagascar	12.4	40.0	5.9	18.6	1.2	1.6	..	5.5	0.3	1.5	..	..
Mixed exporters	*143.4*	*234.2*	*16.8*	*49.9*	*3.0*	*5.3*	..	*21.2*	*4.9*	*12.5*	..	*2.3*
Benin	49.1	122.8	..	..	1.0	3.3	..	10.5	..	3.8	..	0.2
Burkina Faso	..	..	..	..	..	..	..	13.4	..	..	..	0.3
Burundi	12.0	27.4	2.1	5.6	1.5	2.2	..	7.2	0.0	0.6	..	0.8
Cameroon	1.1	54.0	3.6	16.9	0.5	1.5	..	14.8	0.3	2.0	..	0.6
Central African Republic	..	30.3	0.6	0.6	0.3	0.8	..	3.3	0.0	0.7	..	0.2
Egypt	..	363.6	..	76.5	3.8	4.6	..	9.7	2.7	9.1	..	0.4
Eritrea	..	..	..	..	..	..	..	..	..	..	..	..
Ghana	..	339.4	27.5	34.8	3.1	5.4	..	29.4	..	4.3	..	0.9
Kenya	103.4	523.9	20.1	77.8	2.7	4.9	..	42.3	1.6	8.9	..	13.4
Morocco	..	..	..	..	9.9	21.5	..	39.1	8.3	20.8	..	2.8
Mozambique	..	..	3.8	23.8	1.8	3.4	..	39.9	1.8	5.9	..	1.3
Namibia	98.5	471.8	32.7	109.8	7.7	7.4	..		..	39.7	..	..
Niger	..	..	..	..	..	..	..	1.5	..	..	..	0.4
Senegal	..	..	..	..	..	..	..	5.8	..	..	..	0.2
Sierra Leone	..	154.6	3.4	11.8	1.2	2.8	..	15.3	..	0.4	..	0.7
South Africa	..	..	..	..	4.8	10.1	..	53.6	29.9	57.2	..	4.4
Swaziland	370.0	521.3	79.1	156.7	6.3	6.7	..	28.6	7.5	24.4	..	4.7
Togo	82.8	202.8	..	..	1.5	4.2	..	10.2	..	..	..	0.4
Uganda	87.1	179.5	..	17.5	1.1	2.4	..	20.5	1.1	3.6	..	3.3
United Republic of Tanzania	..	..	9.6	31.4	1.2	1.9	..	17.3	0.3	6.6	..	5.5
Zimbabwe	486.3	105.0	2.4	14.5	2.7	5.7	..	39.7	..	5.5	..	2.6
World	*359.2*	*589.2*	*111.5*	*180.2*	*17.6*	*19.0*	..	*45.2*	*32.8*	*42.9*	..	*3.2*
Africa total	*169.2*	*283.2*	*28.3*	*52.3*	*4.2*	*6.8*	..	*21.5*	*4.8*	*11.1*	..	*3.3*
East Asia and Pacific	*581.8*	*695.4*	*200.4*	*235.8*	*14.5*	*14.6*	..	*54.9*	*29.8*	*40.8*	..	*2.4*
Latin America and Caribbean	*524.8*	*736.2*	*138.4*	*233.8*	*15.8*	*21.9*	..	*34.1*	*27.5*	*41.8*	..	*1.4*
South Asia	*426.6*	*462.0*	*78.0*	*57.6*	*7.9*	*10.2*	..	*31.3*	*1.9*	*8.4*	..	*1.4*
Other developing countries	*563.8*	*642.9*	*214.1*	*162.6*	*14.8*	*14.9*	..	*42.7*	*21.7*	*33.6*	..	*5.4*

Source: UNCTAD secretariat calculations based, on data from the *World Development Indicators* (World Bank, 2014) and *Global Finance Development* database, February 2015.

Improving access to finance for SMEs and poor households that are currently excluded may require State intervention, through regulation or direct provision by State-owned development finance institutions, as market-led processes may not be sufficient in some countries.

Kenya's Equity Bank and M-PESA are good examples of banks successfully improving access to finance in rural and urban areas to the unbanked. Indeed, these banks and the financial and technological innovations that they have deployed to increase access and outreach are extending the financial mainstream to the unbanked. Indeed, there is some evidence that many of the traditional services banks provide (credit, payments, money storage) are being unbundled and sold separately. For example new forms of remittance service provider firms are emerging that allow people to transfer funds using pipelines that bypass banks and other traditional intermediaries and reduce fees in the process. Nonetheless, most of the poor have scant access to financial services such as savings and insurance products. Microlenders still have an important role to play in providing basic financial services, but many Governments can also do more by encouraging innovation and helping banks to deal with regulatory hurdles that constrain access to finance, especially for SMEs. Measures might include making more State benefits such as pensions available electronically and providing official identification cards to make it easier for banks to verify the identity of potential customers, thereby easing the access of the poor to financial services.

Figure 7 shows that about 22 per cent of small firms acquired a formal loan in 2011, despite 86 per cent of these firms having a formal bank account, either a savings or checking account. In proportionate terms, the medium and large firms do slightly better. Across all three size groups defined by the number of employees, enterprises in African countries are less likely to have a loan than other developing countries, with large firms in Africa even less likely to have a loan than medium-sized firms outside Africa. Almost two thirds of small firms in Africa lack access to formal sources of finance. The lack of finance available from African banks to SMEs is due in part to a reluctance to lend to them and a tendency to adopt risk-adverse lending strategies. The capacity of SMEs to invest is to some extent determined by these tight credit constraints.

In many enterprise surveys, access to credit and the relatively high costs of finance in Africa are often cited as key constraints to the growth of SMEs (Aghion et al., 2007). Also, at the sectoral level the agricultural sector suffers most from acute financing and investment constraints because of overstretched legal systems

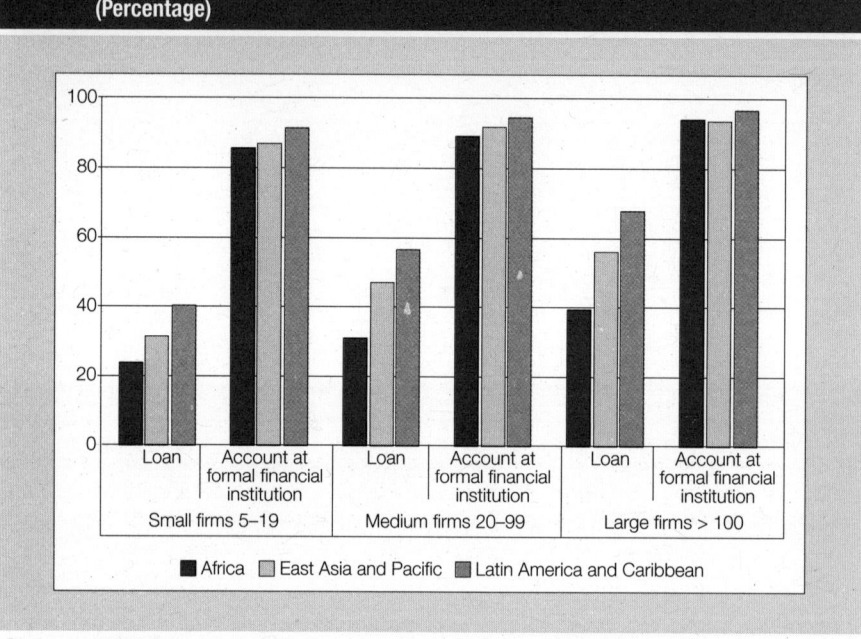

Figure 7. Use of formal account and loan services across firm-size groups, 2011 (Percentage)

Source: UNCTAD secretariat calculations, based on data from G20 Financial Inclusion Indicators Database.

Note: Denotes the percentage of small (5–19 employees), medium (20–99 employees) or large (> 100 employees) enterprises with a checking or savings account.

and weak property rights systems for land and capital equipment, making the collateralization of loans difficult (UNCTAD, 2009).

In terms of financial access and outreach, African countries have fewer depositors with commercial banks (on average 283 per 1,000) than most other developing countries (642.9 per 1,000) with double the number of depositors.

Africa also has among the lowest number of commercial bank branches (seven per 100,000 adults) in the world. Table 14 shows that there is a large variation in the number of commercial bank branches, ranging from the Seychelles with 46 per 100,000 adults, to the Central African Republic, Chad and the Democratic Republic of the Congo, with one branch per 100,000 adults. The number of depositors and borrowers with commercial banks has risen since 2004. With the onset of the global financial crisis of 2008–2009, lending conditions tightened, and the number of borrowers declined slightly.

African countries average 11.1 automated teller machines (ATMs) per 100,000 adults, compared with 33.6 in other developing countries. South Africa, the Seychelles and Mauritius have four to five times the average number of ATMs in Africa per 100,000 adults (see table 14).

Mobile money and remittance transfer payments systems are evolving, and new channels and technologies are emerging. From 1995 to 2005, mobile phone subscribers increased from zero to 88 million and by 2010 had reached 360 million subscribers (Visa sub-Saharan Africa, 2013). This may compensate for a lower number of commercial bank branches. In most of Africa there remains little interoperability between ATM and point of sale networks, which limits customer numbers and therefore the financial viability of these networks. Most bank branch and ATM networks are located in major population centres, which limits rural access. With improving infrastructure and the growth of mobile bank branches, branchless banking, and rural clientele access to financial services should improve, given the sharp increase of mobile phone use for financial services. Interactive connectivity in Africa is rapidly growing, creating greater potential for access to finance, for example, mobile money services, and low-cost mobile microinsurance and savings products. However, regulatory issues have arisen as a result of concerns at the international level about money laundering (IMF, 2014). Smartcard and wireless technologies are enabling the development of services being offered in previously unbanked areas and consumers. Mobile money is, however, not a panacea for financial inclusion, as it still accounts for a smaller value of transactions than traditional instruments (Jack and Suri, 2011).

C. INTERNATIONALIZATION OF BANKING: CROSS-BORDER BANKING

This section explores the development in the internationalization of banking and in particular cross-border banking in the context of financial services liberalization. The development of cross-border banking in Africa is in some ways the actual realization or not of the commitments discussed later with regard to GATS modes 3 and 4. This section briefly considers cross-border banking and its regulation in Africa.

Over the past two decades, the banking systems of Africa have undergone significant structural changes, such as the creation of regional banking commissions in francophone Africa and improved supervision of counterparty risk at most commercial banks (Beck et al., 2009; Kasekende, 2010). Similarly, since the bank privatization and financial liberalization trends of the 1980s, the ownership structure of Africa's banks has undergone significant transformation, with foreign banks dominating in some countries and only a few banking systems with largely State-owned banks. For example, in 2009, foreign bank assets as a share of total bank assets in Africa was 58 per cent; the OECD (34 members) equivalent was 38 per cent.

Similarly, figure 8 shows that by 2009, foreign banks accounted for 52 per cent of all commercial banks in Africa. The trend towards greater foreign bank ownership in the African banking sector has almost doubled since 1995, rising from about 120 banks to 227 by 2009. Hence, foreign bank penetration in terms of both ownership and bank assets is comparatively much higher in Africa than in other regions.

There is inevitably some arbitrariness about any threshold of ownership, but identifying banks as foreign only if ownership is greater than 50 per cent may be problematic. For example, Ecobank could be identified as South African on that basis. Hence, ownership and corporate strategy are complex, and foreignness does not imply a pre-determined pattern of behaviour that is either good or bad for development. It is also important to note that ownership is not the only route to improving banking competitiveness in foreign markets. What is important is the increasing trend in cross-border banking in Africa and its effects on and implications for financial intermediation and financial services regulation.

Foreign bank ownership in Africa can be grouped into two categories:

(a) International banks from outside Africa, usually from Europe but also increasingly South–South banks from emerging economies such as India and China;

(b) African cross-border banks incorporated in African continental jurisdictions where the main players are Kenya, Morocco, Nigeria and South Africa.

The share of African foreign-owned cross-border commercial banks between 1995 and 2009 rose by 12 percentage points from 15 to 27 per cent. During the same period, the share of foreign-owned (non-African) banks in Africa increased by 4 percentage points from 24 to 28 per cent. The rate of growth of African cross-border banks outstripped foreign (non-African) bank ownership in Africa especially in Uganda, Burundi and Senegal. Algeria, Egypt, Mozambique and Zambia have witnessed the highest rates of growth in foreign (non-African) bank ownership. Underlying these trends are large variations. For example, many African

---

Figure 8. Number and share of domestic and foreign banks, 1995–2009

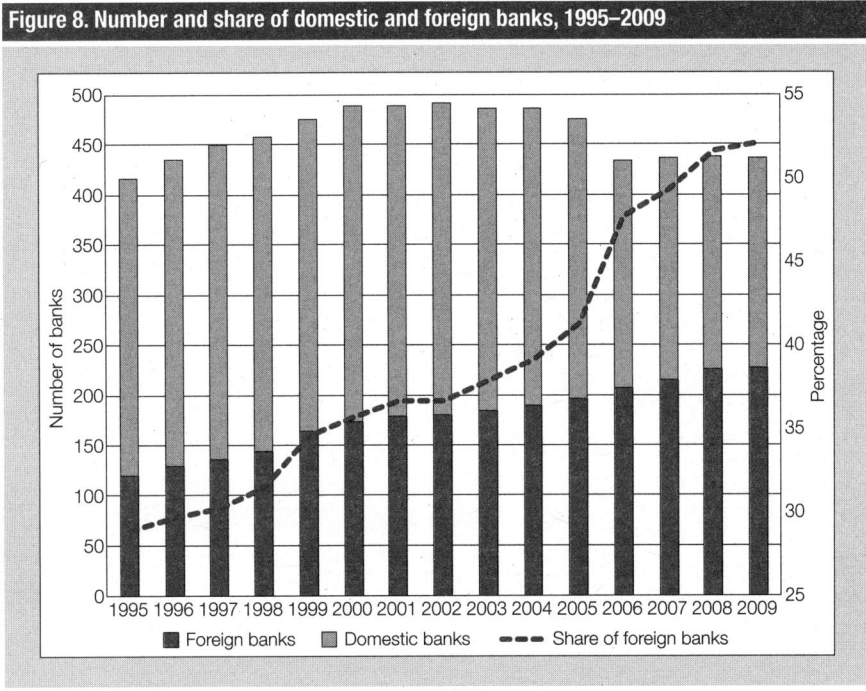

Source: UNCTAD secretariat calculations, based on data from Claessens and Horen, 2014.
Note: Covers full ownership data from 1995 to 2009 of all commercial banks, saving banks, bank holding companies and cooperative banks (as identified in Bankscope) that are currently or have been active in 36 African countries. Bank ownership is defined as foreign if more than 50 per cent of shares are held by foreigners. Unless otherwise specified, ownership reflects direct ownership. Only banks that are or have been reporting to Bankscope are included.

countries have banking systems dominated by domestic banks, such as Ethiopia (100 per cent), Nigeria and South Africa (80 per cent). On the other hand, in some countries such as Burkina Faso and Madagascar, there are only foreign-owned banks. Mozambique has less than 10 per cent domestically owned banks and the ECOWAS region has many banks operating from neighbouring countries.

What are the driving forces underpinning the trends presented in figure 8. These trends show that between 2006 and 2009 there is a period of consolidation, with the number of domestic banks in Africa declining, compared with the period 2000–2005, and the rate of foreign banks slowing after 2007. This decline can be attributed to a combination of bank-specific and home- and host-country factors.

Since 2000, there has been a rise in the integration of financial services by way of consolidation within and across financial services subsectors and M&A. In Africa, greater financial sector opening-up and internationalization has led to a drive to enhance competitiveness, efficiency and economies of scale, and to grow market share through M&A. In the light of the 2008–2009 crisis, several banks in European countries have been forced into liquidation, or were on the verge of bankruptcy, leading to heightened M&A activity. Since the financial crisis, there has been a trend towards both greater cross-border activity and consolidation in the sector.

Table 15 provides a simplified classification of the major cross-border and international banks in Africa, as both a bank's headquarters and shareholding may change over time. From a banking regulatory perspective, the criteria used to determine a bank's home supervisor is generally the ownership structure (Beck et al., 2013). Most of the major international banks active in cross-border banking in Africa reflect strong economic and political ties with former colonial powers such as France (Société Générale) and the United Kingdom of Great Britain and Northern Ireland (Standard Chartered) and have expanded operations beyond their colonial connections. The United States Citigroup Bank has in recent decades established a presence in Africa by expanding its branch network and opening subsidiaries across the continent.

The rise in pan-African or perhaps more accurately South–South banking enables African banks to exploit local and regional knowledge in designing appropriate services and products for their widening clientele. For example, Ecobank Africa's biggest lender by geographic reach provides financial services in 32 African countries (see table 15). It was started as an international bank and provides innovative retail, corporate and investment banking services and is one of the continent's fastest growing banks. Ecobank's growth has also been driven through consolidation and M&A of other banks. Similarly, South Africa's Standard Bank, Africa's top lender by assets, currently operates in 18 African countries (see table 15). In 2008, the Industrial Commercial Bank of China bought a 20 per cent stake in Standard Bank, leaving the former well placed to take advantage of Asia's growing presence in Africa.

Although there is a rising presence of major foreign banks and their subsidiaries in Africa, these institutions have tended to focus on high-margin businesses, such as consulting services on M&A and asset-backed finance; and corporate and trade financing. The unbanked, for example, women, SMEs, and the rural and urban poor, have been largely excluded from recent developments in more sophisticated

Table 15. Major cross-border and international banks, 2013

Cross-border banks			
Name	Number of African countries	Location of headquarters	Majority ownership
Ecobank	32	Togo	South Africa
United Bank for Africa (UBA)	19	Nigeria	Nigeria
Standard Bank Group (Stanbic)	18	South Africa	South Africa
Banque Marocaine du Commerce Extérieur (BMCE)	18	Morocco	Morocco
Société Générale	17	France	France
Citigroup	15	United States	United States
Standard Chartered	15	United Kingdom	United Kingdom
Banque Sahélo Saharienne pour l'Investissement et le Commerce (BSIC)	14	Libya	Libya
BNP Paribas	13	France	France
Attijariwafa Bank	12	Morocco	Morocco
International banks			
Name	Number of African countries	Location of headquarters	Majority ownership
Société Générale	17	France	France
Citigroup	15	United States	United States
Standard Chartered	14	United Kingdom	United Kingdom
BNP Paribas	13	France	France
Bank of Baroda	9	India	India
Access Holding	5	Germany	Unknown
Albaraka Bank (Group)	5	Bahrain	Bahrain
HBL Pakistan (Habib Bank Ltd.)	5	Pakistan	United Rep. of Tanzania
International Commercial Bank (ICB)	5	Switzerland	Malaysia
Rabobank	5	Netherlands	Netherlands

Source: Beck et al., (2014); Claessens et al., 2014; bank websites and annual reports.
Notes: Number of countries includes home country (if African) and representation through subsidiaries or branches in African countries; representative offices are not included.

financial service products and provision. Most foreign-owned commercial banks have used variations of the same basic business model, focusing on serving wealthy consumers, Government ministries and large firms (Claessens and Van Horen, 2014). Retail banking remains a largely untapped market and provides scope for greater expansion and competition on service quality and products. As long as Europe remains in recession, it is likely that international banks will continue to expand their operations in Africa in the short to medium term.

Another means of assessing the magnitude and growth of cross-border banking activity is to consider bank loans and deposits with non-residents. The rapid growth of outstanding cross-border loans and deposits from 2000 until the onset of the 2008–2009 financial crisis was interrupted by a retrenchment in the following years, but the positive trend in international banking has since resumed. As of June 2011, seven countries (France, Germany, Greece, Ireland, Italy, Portugal and Spain) accounted for $61 billion of the $200 billion cross-border lending from Europe to Africa (World Bank, 2012). South Africa received around 20 per cent of these flows, Liberia 16 per cent, Mauritius 12 per cent and Angola, Morocco and Nigeria, 7 per cent each.

Constraints on cross-border banking and impact on development

The most significant constraint on cross-border banking is probably the limited availability of inputs, especially low levels of capabilities in host country financial markets for essential tasks such as credit evaluation and risk management. But ICT skills are also in short supply. Well-known deficiencies in physical infrastructure provision of electricity supply and communications hamper financial services by creating bottlenecks and service interruptions, requiring banks to insure themselves against this by providing their own supply at high cost. Mobile telephony has substantially expanded access to financial services for consumers, and reduced operational and transactional costs. Indeed, the success of Equity Bank, Commercial Bank of Africa in East Africa and UBA of Nigeria has depended on the capitalization of mobile phone access to reduce the operational costs of banking.

Skill and capability shortages limit the number of banks with the potential to operate across-borders, even in neighbouring economies within the continent. This is intensified by the small size of most African banks, that is, low capitalization and limited balance sheets, which restricts expansion. With the exception of BMCE and Attijariwafa banks, most of the regional banks have more direct entry presence than alliances in regional countries. Cross-border alliances among banks are few and may have far smaller benefits for development than foreign entry, owing to fewer technology transfer effects, and reduces the competition-enhancing impact of new bank entry into a national market (Bleeke and Ernst, 1991).

Further, regulatory limitations and shortcomings are common in Africa. These include poor accounting and auditing standards and practices, and weak legal systems, resulting in poor rule of law and contract enforcement. Both of these are likely to restrict foreign banks' appetite for business loans in foreign markets with which they are less familiar. In addition, there are risks of financial instability and contagion because of weak financial regulation and supervision in many African economies. Problems include the lack of harmonization of banking supervision standards and requirements across jurisdictions, and regulatory skills shortages leading to a lack of capability to supervise across borders or across financial services subsectors, or to maintain oversight of outsourced activities. For many foreign banks, this may be a disincentive to entry, as weak or inconsistent regulation could undermine their potential competitive advantages in the host market as a result of inconsistent treatment of foreign and national firms.

D. FINANCIAL SERVICES AND CROSS-BORDER BANKING REGULATION

National and pan-African financial services regulation

This chapter is less about financial service liberalization per se in the sense of financial deregulation and capital account liberalization; it focuses more on the implications of further opening up the financial services sector to trade with foreign suppliers. Since the financial crisis of 2008–2009, it has become clear that many developing countries have greater concerns about the process of financial liberalization and the extent to which it will foster greater financial inclusion or yield tangible economic benefits for their countries (Bellmann, 2014). Opening up to financial services trade in the absence of appropriate domestic regulations may not necessarily increase trade or generate greater efficiency in the provision of financial services. The financial crisis struck at the heart of the international financial system and affected most multinational banking groups (Acharya and Schnabl, 2010). Many of these banks took excessive risks before the financial crisis and exploited countries' commitments to liberalizing trade in financial services to engage in regulatory arbitrage. Since the crisis, there has been a gradual reappraisal of the evidence on the stability implications of financial sector liberalization and multinational banking (UNCTAD, 2011). Clearly, financial markets need regulation, limits and surveillance in order to make market failures less frequent and less costly.

Domestic financial sector supervision and regulation must be enhanced

Domestic financial services and cross-border supervision and regulation are critical and are improving in Africa. The legal and regulatory environment plays a pivotal role in the efficient functioning of the financial sector. African policymakers also recognize the importance of improving the domestic regulatory environment for the financial sector and related market infrastructures. Regulatory differences in the responsibilities of home-country supervisors (ensure solvency of the banking group) and of host-country supervisors (ensure that there is sufficient liquidity to meet all obligations and protect depositors) can lead to both overlaps and gaps in the regulatory framework applicable to a cross-border bank. This can generate serious regulatory coordination problems, requiring the creation of cross-border supervisory and crisis management groups for systemically important banks.

Given the growing internationalization of banking and the recent experience of the global financial crisis, the emerging regulatory environment needs to better incorporate mechanisms for crisis prevention and resolution. In Africa, there remains scope for better domestic regulation of the financial sector in the provision of clear supervisory guidance to help improve domestic banks' risk management and stress-testing frameworks. These initiatives should also include regional shocks into stress-test scenarios. Central bank authorities and policymakers may also need to increase efforts aimed at monitoring and handling bank balance sheet mismatches, for example those arising from foreign currency funding, while avoiding an imbalance between the potential costs and benefits of any associated regulatory measures such as constraints on certain types of funding. In some countries, there will also be a need for regulatory authorities to address constraints on the ability of banks to better hedge their balance sheet risks by helping to improve local markets for bonds and related hedging instruments.

The regulatory environment for preventing potential financial system crises, bank failures and resolution regimes for financial institutions will require greater efforts at regional coordination to better address potential spillover effects. Regional coordination and arrangements will need to be put into place to both strengthen existing safety nets and enhance existing regulatory frameworks such as supervisory colleges and regional forums. For example, the Financial

Stability Board Regional Consultative Group for Sub-Saharan Africa, comprising African financial sector policymakers and supervisors, meets to discuss ways to increasingly synchronize monetary conditions and regulatory frameworks. This process includes engaging with its non-African counterparts and reaching out to countries that are not represented in the regional consultative groups. UNCTAD analysis of data of meetings of the Regional Consultative Group from 2012 to 2014 shows that issues such as the resilience and stability of financial institutions and the effective supervision of systemically important financial institutions are of prime concern and most frequently referred to. Also, at the bi-monthly meetings of central bank governors at the Bank for International Settlements, there is a regular Africa session where regional representatives gather to discuss themes of special relevance to their economies.

Despite some progress, most African banking systems continue to be small and costly in terms of overheads, lacking the scale required to significantly reduce the cost of their services. Promoting cross-border banking and implementing regulatory coordination measures to address emerging challenges has the potential to promote growth through deeper regional integration. Regional and subregional integration is a key condition for achieving economies of scale. The regional integration of finance and regulatory frameworks is gradually developing in Africa. For example, in 2013, the SADC Integrated Regional Electronic Settlement System, commonly known by its acronym SIRESS, was successfully implemented in the four countries of the Common Monetary Area: South Africa, Namibia, Lesotho and Swaziland. Similarly, in 2010, EAC initiated the process of harmonizing payment systems by setting up the East African Payment System (Economic Commission for Africa, African Union and African Development Bank, 2010).

Regional integration and the existence of several currency unions in Africa, the Common Monetary Area and the CFA zones in francophone Africa, also have potentially important implications for financial services and for financial services trade. Despite the importance of this, there is relatively little empirical research on the issue. Wakeman-Linn and Wagh (2008) found that financial integration contributes significantly to the strengthening and development of Africa's financial market if two conditions are present: (a) that there is political commitment to the integration process and effective independent regulatory bodies; and (b) there is a broad commitment to deepening economic integration and to the provision of adequate financial resources to building the necessary institutions and infrastructure.

Frey and Volz (2011) examined the effects of political agreements concerning regional financial integration in Africa on financial market development and access to and cost of finance. They found that regional financial integration positively affects financial development (measured as the size of the financial sector, including the liabilities of the central banks) when combined with a sufficient level of institutional quality. Both Wakeman-Linn and Wagh (2008) and Frey and Volz (2011) identify one caveat concerning the implications of regional financial integration for financial development, namely that unless institutional quality is improved, combined with adequate political commitment, access to financial services will continue to be inadequate for the unbanked and SMEs. As African Governments increase efforts to deepen integration with the CFTA, they will also need to develop in tandem a more robust regulatory framework for the financial sector.

Given the rising prevalence of cross-border banking, countries will need to consider establishing bank-specific supervisory colleges for Africa's largest cross-border banks. They will also need to strengthen national and regional cross-border supervisory practices. This will require improved central bank coordination, resolution frameworks and stronger burden-sharing arrangements. In order to resist future financial crises, this is particularly important as Africa's internationalization of banks and deeper integration into global financial markets continues. This may require greater pan-African coordination and monitoring of those countries and banks where systemic cross-border risks are identified. For example, the Community of African Banking Supervisors could perhaps play a greater role managing and coordinating this process.

Cross-border banking regulation and supervision

The international regulatory and supervisory context matters for enhanced financial stability in Africa. Since 2012, emerging debates concerning GATS and the Trade in Services Agreement have tended to divert attention from the need to incorporate and regulate financial inclusion. These factors are not featured in the mandate of the Bank for International Settlements and other financial supervisory bodies. It is also worth noting that international initiatives to promote financial inclusion are not legally binding. Global Standard-Setting Bodies and Financial Inclusion for the Poor: Toward Proportionate Standards and Guidance (Global Partnership for Financial Inclusion, 2011) and Principles for Investors in Inclusive Finance are examples of non-binding initiatives. With several foreign banks operating in Africa, the impact on financial inclusion practices could be serious if these banks fail, reminiscent of what occurred during the recent global financial crisis, and if they lead to greater financial exclusion.

The globalization of finance, shaped by trade and investment agreements, national policies and corporate strategies has encouraged greater and perhaps more intense competition in the financial sector leading to financial sector business models that tend to serve the wealthier clients and larger firms. As foreign banks dominate the sector in many African countries, this is changing the portfolio of credit and services offered and business strategies pursued such as "cherry picking" the most profitable services, which usually excludes rural clientele. There could however be greater scope for local and State banks to offer services to rural areas, women and SMEs.

Nonetheless, more African States will need to enhance their capacity to regulate cross-border banking. For example, Ecobank's corporate governance problems that emerged in 2014 and severely shook confidence in the Bank has provided a critical test for central bank regulators tasked with developing effective cross-border supervision (Financial Times, 2014a). Insufficient cross-border supervision and lower regulatory standards in some frontier markets are constraints on the ratings of pan-African banking groups. Consolidated supervision of cross-border banking groups in Africa would encourage a more cohesive approach to risk management and regulation, and reduce corporate governance risks. The investigation in 2014 of Ecobank by Nigeria's Securities and Exchange Commission has shown how the crisis at the holding company, which falls outside the regulatory purview of the Commission, could by association undermine confidence in a broader banking-sector recovery. There was great concern about the risks that a run on the Nigerian subsidiary might have and pose elsewhere, as it represents 40 per cent of a business spread across 32 African countries (Financial Times, 2014b).

Therefore, African banks should aim to implement the Basel Core Principles for Effective Banking Supervision as they pertain to cross-border activities (Bank for International Settlements, 2012). The standards, developed by the Basel Committee, constitute non-legally binding minimum standards mainly aimed at internationally active banks. It contains 29 principles focusing on powers, responsibilities and functions of supervisors of banks as well as on prudential regulation[15] and bank supervision. For example, principle 12 highlights the importance of supervising banking groups on a consolidated basis. The principle requires supervisors to monitor and apply prudential standards to all aspects of the business conducted by a banking group worldwide. This obligation includes reviewing whether the oversight of a bank's foreign operations by management of the parent bank is sufficient.

In the context of these principles, recent experience in supervising and regulating cross-border banking in Africa has been varied and largely non-compliant. The World Bank and IMF assess countries' compliance with the principles in the context of financial sector assessment programmes, which include financial sector stability assessments. Beck et al. (2014) surveyed the compliance of 18 assessed African supervisory authorities between 2006 and 2013 with the key Basel principles and categorized them as compliant, largely compliant, materially non-compliant or non-compliant. The results show them to be largely compliant with the Basel core principles. However, Beck et al (2014) note that these standards have been raised since the global financial crisis. The findings also show that most African supervisory authorities failed to comply with principle 12; further, 11 African countries were non-compliant. However, strict adherence to some of these accords (for example on capital adequacy) in an already financially constrained environment could be counterproductive and stifle the growth of financial institutions and access to credit.

Cross-border banking supervision and regulation is particularly challenging for a number of reasons. First, Africa's high level of financial heterogeneity makes regional regulators adopt a lowest-common-denominator approach to supervision. Second, the lack of incentives for host and home supervisors to share information and the absence of binding regional regulations hinder effective cross-border supervision. Third, in some countries, political constraints may inhibit cross-border cooperation and deeper regional integration. Although cross-border cooperation on financial services cannot be enforced at the regional level, positive steps are being taken to address this through information-sharing forums.

E. GLOBAL REGULATORY COMMITMENTS ON FINANCIAL SERVICES TRADE

African member States have made important financial services commitments at the global level in the context of the General Agreement on Trade in Services.

African countries have been engaged in financial services liberalization in the context of GATS under the aegis of WTO since its establishment in 1995. As previously noted, financial services represent the third most committed services sector in African GATS schedules, after tourism and business services. A total of

20 African member States have made important commitments in return for market access in the 160-plus members of WTO, representing virtually half of the Africa Group. Table 16 summarizes the main features of the schedules of commitments as they pertain to financial services in its two main subcategories: banking and other financial services, and insurance services.

Commitments on financial services portray a high level of variability across African countries in terms of coverage and depth.

Twenty African countries have made commitments that are specific to the banking and other financial services subcategory, while a smaller subgroup of 15 countries made commitments relating to insurance services. A total of 14 countries have inscribed horizontal commitments that affect all sectors, including financial services, whereas only 8 countries have carved out MFN exemptions, which apply to either all sectors or are specific to financial services. From the aforementioned group of 20 countries, Angola, Benin, Gabon, Mozambique and Zimbabwe are the only ones that have exclusively undertaken sectoral commitments in financial services and have made no commitments in the horizontal and MFN exemption sections of their schedules. Swaziland has carved out an MFN exemption in financial services without a sectoral or horizontal commitment in place. The remaining countries have covered financial services more comprehensively, scheduling horizontal commitments and/or MFN exemptions in addition to their sectoral commitments. In particular, Cabo Verde, Egypt, Mauritius, Sierra Leone and South Africa are among the most prolific, with commitments in the three sections of their schedules. In almost all countries, the majority of the horizontal commitments affecting all sectors include financial services and mainly modes 3 and 4. These pertain primarily to requirements or limitations on land and firm ownership, entry and temporary stay of business persons, as well as foreign personnel requirements, and certification and accreditation requirements. The schedules of Lesotho, Ghana and Morocco also include modes 1 and 2, but in large part bear no limitations, as "none" is inscribed, meaning that foreign banks can offer financial services such as electronic banking and the holding of bank accounts for foreign private persons.

There are two types of MFN exemptions that affect financial services: first, those which are afforded cross-sectorally for all the services sectors inscribed in a schedule, and second, those which are exclusive to financial services. The first type of exemption is found in the schedules of Cabo Verde, Egypt and Sierra Leone. These mainly deal with waivers on existing limitations or mode 4 requirements for services providers, depending on their nationality and on the extension of full national treatment to nationals of countries that are members of regional economic communities. These exemptions respond to the desire to maintain historical ties, observe regional integration obligations or ensure reciprocity with main trading partners. The second type of exemption is found in the schedules of Côte d'Ivoire, Mauritius, Senegal, South Africa and Swaziland and relates to waivers conferring preferential treatment specifically to financial services providers in mode 3 and 4, either on the basis of regional integration obligations or reciprocity. Turning to the scope of the sectoral commitments for financial services in African schedules and what it means for foreign commercial banking activity in Africa, table 17 summarizes the measures inscribed in the schedules that affect commercial presence and movement of persons, that is to say, modes 3 and 4. These two modes are conduits for investment and employment decisions of foreign banking activity in a given market and can influence the decision of a foreign bank seeking local presence abroad. There are a total of 117 sectoral commitments on financial services, of which 88 pertain to market access and 29 to national treatment limitations. In all, 47 commitments have been inscribed for mode 3 and 70 for mode 4.

Most commitments on financial services in the African schedules translate into limitations or restrictions on ownership and controls of investment and employment decisions of foreign banking activity.

In the case of financial services, most limitations in mode 3 applicable to foreign commercial banks include authorization and licensing requirements, as well as limitations on the form, amount or control of the investment an institution would incur to establish operations through an office. These are critical limitations to banking activity, as they set pre-establishment conditions and limit the capacity of the investing bank to make decisions over the management and control of its investment and operations. For example, Côte d'Ivoire requires that banks be set up as closed-end joint stock companies. According to Benin, Senegal and Tunisia, banks need to be established as a public limited company. Cabo Verde requires that commercial presence take the form of a limited liability company, whereas Sierra Leone requires that subsidiaries be incorporated, and Egypt and Zimbabwe put caps on foreign equity participation in financial institutions. Less frequent are limitations or restrictions of commercial banks participating in equity investment either in the banking or non-banking sector that are also present in mode 3, as well as limitations on the transfer of money or borrowing or lending money to and from the local banking sector. Examples of these are found in the schedules of Kenya, Lesotho, Zimbabwe, South Africa and Morocco, and refer to caps or prohibitions on investment and authorization for transfers and foreign currency operations.

Prudential regulation, which is critical to ensure financial soundness, figures less prominently and only in a few African schedules of commitments.

An important element of market access for foreign banks pertains to prudential regulation in the host country's market, because it sets limitations on financial exposure decisions banks may take, as it is crucial to ensuring financial soundness in a financial system. However, prudential regulation is rarely cited as a limitation in most African schedules. Of the 20 countries with sectoral commitments, only 6 have included express limitations in the form of prudential regulation under mode 3. Ghana, for example, makes reference to the observance of prudential regulations, while Egypt, Sierra Leone, South Africa and Tunisia mention capital requirements, and Mauritius makes reference to criteria for credit exposure of lending activities. In turn, limitations in mode 4 mainly have a bearing on the employment decisions pertaining to the physical presence of managers, senior executive and experts and specialists of banks. All countries have inscribed such limitations in their schedules, with the exception of Angola and Senegal. Some countries such as Egypt also require labour market tests, while the Gambia, Sierra Leone and Zimbabwe require that expatriates for management and expert jobs only be approved if no qualified person is found in the domestic market. Finally, Ghana and Lesotho require training in higher skills for their nationals so that domestic expertise may be developed. With regard to the level of restrictiveness, most countries have numerous and elaborate limitations, especially on market access, that allow them to discriminate against foreign services providers on an MFN basis. This favours domestic commercial banks and makes it difficult for foreign banks to compete and enter the local market. In countries where some level of access is offered to foreign banks, national treatment restrictions may still afford domestic banks an advantage.

Nonetheless, a few countries have lower levels of restrictions, such as Mozambique, which requires foreign banks to abide by the domestic rules and regulations that govern investment and operations in the local banking sector. Angola, Kenya, Malawi, Morocco and Nigeria also appear to have similar restrictions, equating requirements to what is provided for in national laws which regulate the sector or simply portraying the term "none" for no restrictions in mode 3. In view of the coverage and scope of African schedules of commitments for the financial services sector, an important question arises. Does the level of restrictiveness of measures contained in these schedules de facto apply? Some studies have attempted to compare the level of restrictiveness contained in the schedules with reality, with inconclusive results (Barth et al., 2013; Páez, 2008b; Tamirisa et al., 2003). The reality for Africa remains mixed at best.

Figure 9. Financial services trade restrictions index scores, 2012

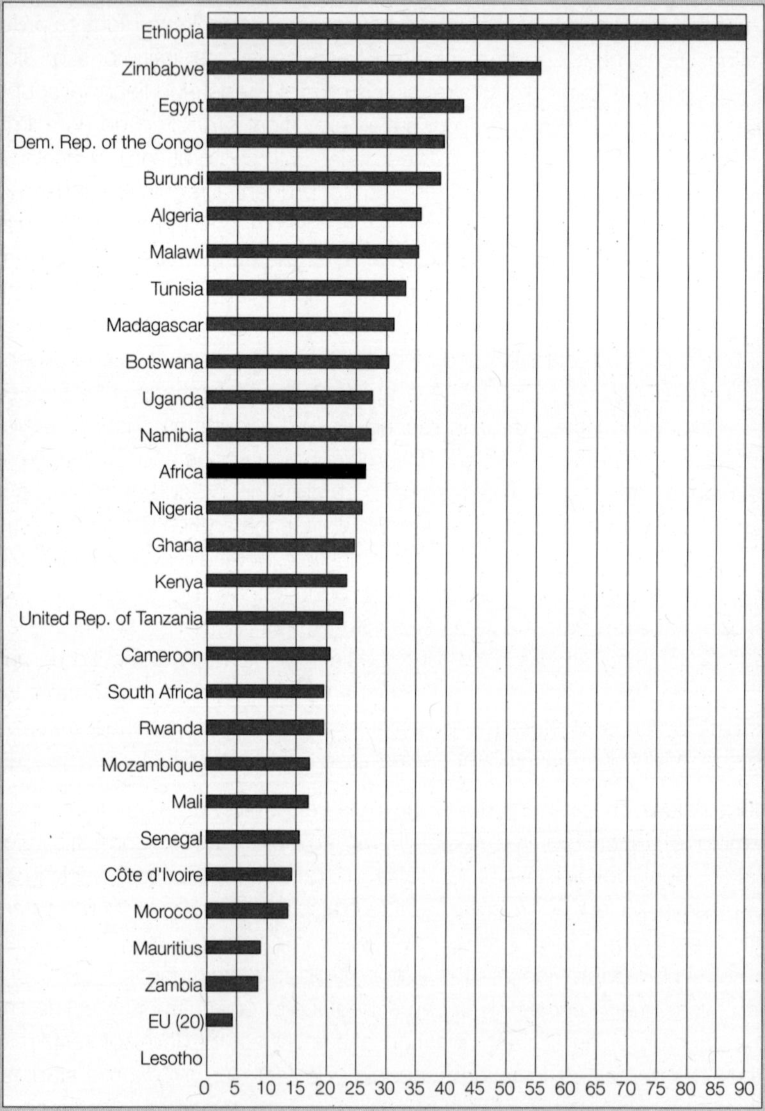

Source: UNCTAD secretariat calculations, based on Borchert et al., 2012.
Note: EU (20) refers to the European Union at 20 members.

Table 16. Overview of financial services commitments under the General Agreement on Trade in Services schedules of African member States

Country	Horizontal commitments affecting financial services	Sectoral commitments on financial services	Banking and other financial services excluding insurance	Insurance services	MFN exemptions affecting financial services	All sectors covered	Exclusive to financial services
Angola	•	•	•				
Benin	•	•	•				
Botswana							
Burkina Faso							
Burundi							
Cameroon							
Cabo Verde	•	•	•	•	•		•
Central African Rep.							
Chad							
Congo							
Côte d'Ivoire		•	•	•	•		•
Dem. Rep. of the Congo							
Djibouti							
Egypt	•	•	•	•	•		•
Gabon	•	•	•	•			
Gambia	•	•	•	•			
Ghana	•	•	•	•			
Guinea							
Guinea Bissau							
Kenya	•	•	•	•			
Lesotho	•	•	•	•			
Madagascar							
Malawi	•	•	•				
Mali							
Mauritania							
Mauritius	•	•	•	•	•		•
Morocco	•	•	•	•			
Mozambique		•	•				
Namibia							
Niger							
Nigeria	•	•	•	•			
Rwanda							
Senegal		•	•	•	•		•
Sierra Leone	•	•	•	•	•	•	
South Africa	•	•	•	•	•		•
Swaziland					•		•
Togo							
Tunisia	•	•	•	•			
Uganda							
United Rep. of Tanzania							
Zambia							
Zimbabwe	•	•	•				

Source: Developed by UNCTAD, based on country schedules of commitments. http://i-tip.wto.org/services/Search.aspx (accessed 5 April 2015).

Table 17. Measures affecting investment and employment in banking and financial services of African General Agreement on Trade in Services schedules[a]

Country	Admission, authorization, licensing or notification requirements	Limitations on form, amount or control of foreign direct investment	Limitations to participating in mergers and acquisitions/ privatization	Limitations on lease or purchase of real estate	Limitations on subsidies, tax write-offs, transfers or preferential treatment	Establishment approval, registration or residency requirements	Qualifications, skills or employment requirements	Limitations on employee category or function	Limitations on duration of stay[b]	Economic needs, social benefit or labour market tests
Angola					MA 3					MA 3
Benin	MA 3	MA 3	MA 3			MA 4	MA 4	MA 4		
Cabo Verde	MA 3	MA 3					MA 4	MA 4	MA 4	
Cote d'Ivoire	MA 3	MA 3				MA 4				
Egypt	MA 3, NT 3	MA 3					MA 4			MA 3, NT 3
Gabon	MA 3						MA* 4	MA* 4		
Gambia	MA 3	MA 4				MA 3, MA*4	MA* 4			MA* 4
Ghana	MA 3				NT 3	MA 4	MA 4	MA 4		MA 4
Kenya	MA 3	MA 3	MA 3			MA 4	MA 4	MA 4		
Lesotho	MA 3	MA 3	MA 3				MA 4	MA 4	MA 4	MA 4
Malawi						MA* 4	MA* 4	MA* 4		
Mauritius	MA 3	MA 3	MA 3				MA* 4	MA* 4		
Morocco					MA 4	MA 4	MA 4	MA 4	MA 4	
Mozambique						MA 4				
Nigeria	MA 3	MA 3				MA* 4	MA* 4	MA* 4		
Senegal	NT 3	MA 3								
Sierra Leone	MA 3	MA 3	MA 3		MA 3		MA* 4	MA* 4		MA 4
South Africa	MA 3	MA 3	MA 3		MA 3, NT 3		MA* 4	MA* 4	MA* 4	
Tunisia	MA 3, NT 3					MA 4, NT 3		MA 4, NT 3		
Zimbabwe	MA 3	MA 3	MA 3	MA 3		MA* 4	MA* 4	MA* 4		MA* 4

Source: Developed by UNCTAD, based on country schedules of commitments. http://i-tip.wto.org/services/Search.aspx (accessed 5 April 2015).

Notes: a   Does not cover insurance or insurance-related sectors.

      b   Refers to expressly stated limitations on the number of years, months or days.

      Modes of supply: 3 = commercial presence, 4 = presence of natural persons.

      Abbreviations: MA, market access column; NT, national treatment column; MA*, limitations inscribed in MA also apply to NT modes of supply.

The restrictiveness of trade in financial services varies widely among African countries and is highest in Ethiopia, Zimbabwe and Egypt, which boast well above-average financial services trade restrictions index scores of 26 (figure 9). Zambia, Mauritius and Morocco have among the most open services trade regimes in the world. However, in many African countries, the absence of sectoral regulation can often lead to a low score. Thus financial services trade openness is probably qualitatively different in Africa, compared with other regions. Nonetheless, financial services trade in Africa appears on average to be less restrictive than in other developing regions (Borchert et al., 2012).

F. BALANCING DOMESTIC AND GLOBAL FINANCIAL SERVICES REGULATION

Lack of a regulatory regime limits access and sustainability

Given that the African financial market is underperforming compared to other world regions, foreign banks could have an important role to play in facilitating external finance and in raising the quality of capital through better risk leverage. The presence of foreign bank subsidiaries in African financial markets has increased the availability and quality of financial services, but these improvements remain out of bounds for lower-income households, SMEs and the unbanked sectors of the economy. These banks have not necessarily broadened access to credit or the financial system more generally (World Bank, 2011). Risk management continues to be weaker in Africa, compared with other parts of the world (Mlachila et al., 2013), especially as the sector remains largely focused on financing the public sector and State-owned firms often to the detriment of productive sector financing (Berg and Fuchs, 2013). As the financial sector evolves and becomes increasingly integrated in global financial markets through foreign banking, there are several potential pitfalls that African policymakers and regulators need to avoid and consider when exploring opportunities to harness greater capital flows towards improving productive capacity and economic diversification.

Africa must address structural impediments to finance

Key structural impediments to financial sector development, inclusion and growth include poor infrastructure, monopolies and inadequate regulation of the sector. Many African States still need to introduce policies that foster greater domestic competition and tackle financial market concentration. Greater financial sector diversification and competition through better regulation could also act as a deterrent to external shocks. Although there have been improvements in communications (hence the growth of M-PESA and Equity bank), deficits in energy and transport infrastructure still hold back progress in tackling the chronic undersupply of financial services in rural areas. Regulation can also help address financial market information asymmetries, moral hazard and undersupply to the unbanked, while supporting Government efforts to improve financial inclusion, integrity and stability (see principles for innovative financial inclusion of the Group of 20). Finally, State and development banks also have extensive rural branch networks that can be used to quickly and relatively cheaply extend access to rural financial services.

Africa needs to improve prudential regulation of financial services

An important regulatory aspect for financial services pertains to prudential regulation, which is what regulates the behaviour of banks through capital requirements, lending criteria and other risk exposure criteria so that these do not elicit financial instability. Prudential regulation is critical for the well-being and proper functioning of any financial system, especially to ward off and navigate through financial crises. More generally, prudential regulation can also improve the quality of credit allocation decisions towards those sectors in the economy that are more productive and can therefore report higher returns on investment. The impact of financial crises is a function of information asymmetries and the quality of prudential regulation and authorities. Financial markets tend to be opaque and imperfect, leading to undesirable behaviour by market actors who are in pursuit of better information, such as herding, adverse selection and moral hazard. This tends to skew responses away from sound risk assessment, generating systemic risk and severe liquidity constraints in times of crisis (Eichengreen et al., 1998). Regulation needs therefore to cater for the disclosure of financial information by financial institutions and the establishment of monitoring mechanisms which reliably "read" the market and alert financial authorities about potential systemic risks. Regulations that enhance the disclosure of financial institutions, such as the Basel II and III regulations and the International Accounting Standards, can help discipline financial markets (Baumann and Nier, 2003); foreign banks can improve reporting practices in markets where they establish themselves if they are able to transfer desirable bank governance and risk assessment practices from their country of origin (Buch et al., 2011). African financial markets have managed to steer clear of recent financial crises because they are poorly integrated into global financial markets.

However, as these integration ties deepen through the activity of foreign banks, as well as through the monetization of economic activity, potential contagion effects can quickly spread in the absence of effective prudential regulation. The inadequacy of prudential regulation in Africa also explains insufficient financing of the private sector and can lead to a captive audience of credit institutions for the benefit of the less efficient sectors of the economy and to the detriment of those industries that could report higher productivity gains. In Africa, this is a well-known weakness. For SMEs in particular, access to finance even in countries with strong banking sectors, is relatively constrained. Among the factors explaining this constraint is the extent of Government borrowing (Berg and Fuchs, 2013). Therefore, best practice as mediated through prudential regulation, should allow banks to monitor firms more closely, allocating credit to performing firms, rather than to incumbents. Countries following such practices have been reported to enjoy greater financial depth, which can generate growth through greater allocative efficiency in productive investment (Barth et al., 2013).

Africa must align regional and multilateral regulatory frameworks

In the context of the multilateral trading system, prudential regulation appears to be overlooked in many African GATS schedules of commitments. African countries wishing to regulate the entry of foreign banks should be able to exercise discretion on the basis of their prudential regulation, and since MFN is a major principle for liberalization under GATS, the ability to exercise this discretion may be compromised. Hence, African countries that have yet to liberalize their financial services sector must make sure they use the flexibilities the system has to offer by inscribing prudential carve-outs as MFN exemptions. The definition of these carve-outs will require greater coordination between trade policymakers and central banks, as well as other financial sector authorities and stakeholders.

In addition, African countries will need to extensively examine how to align the sector with existing regional regulation, as some regions already have some protocols in place covering aspects of financial sector integration and/or investment, such as the Arab Maghreb Union, EAC, ECOWAS and SADC, especially as they envisage the free movement of capital in their respective subregions. There is a disconnect between the various existing regional regulations of capital markets; in spite of it, African banks have expanded regional operations. Here too, the formulation of carve-outs will be required to cater for financial integration and the emergence of a regional banking sector, which is developing slowly.

Furthermore, other elements that can be incorporated into the schedules of commitments and which some countries have already used are economic and social needs tests that require foreign banks to facilitate access to the poor and the private sector. This could also be accompanied by requirements on training, better risk assessment and management to ensure that the expected economy-wide effects take root. Lastly, an important element of caution pertains to the potential regulatory encroachment that current negotiations on regional trade agreements covering financial services could bring. African countries are not participating in mega-regional initiatives such as the Trade in Services Agreement and the Transatlantic Trade and Investment Partnership. Both agreements, if endorsed, could imply a financial regulatory encroachment beyond GATS commitments and pre-empt future services liberalization rounds, as they could set a GATS-plus standard in financial services liberalization, well beyond the capacity of many African countries. Therefore, it is critically important that African countries follow these processes closely so that policy processes on financial services are informed of the developments of these agreements with a view to retaining the policy space that has been carved out for financial sector development.

CHAPTER **5**
MAIN FINDINGS
AND RECOMMENDATIONS

A. INTRODUCTION

The story of growth in Africa over the past decade can be partly explained by the remarkable growth in the services sector. The services sector in the continent holds much promise, though the full potential of trade in services is yet to be realized. Services promise to be a vital export sector and an important contributor to total employment, despite a high degree of variation across African economies.

A key policy question, therefore, is how Africa can translate services-led growth into durable employment and greater value addition for its development. Africa is showing immense potential in some of the services subsectors that contribute to trade in goods and, through these subsectors, the continent has an opportunity to link to global value chains. Equally, some countries have managed to develop their services beyond national confines and are supplying these services to other African countries.

In this context, the focus of this report has been to address the major regulatory and policy constraints that frustrate the development of Africa's services trade and how services can help Africa to integrate more beneficially into the world economy and generate growth and development that are sustainable and more inclusive. This chapter recapitulates some of the main findings, key messages and policy recommendations emanating from the report.

B. MAIN FINDINGS

1. Africa's services sector grew at more than twice the world average rate during 2009–2012.

Africa's rapid growth rate in services is comparable to that of the developing world and has a great potential to drive overall growth in the future. During 2009–2012 the services sector in Africa grew at a rate of 4.6 per cent, compared to 5.4 per cent in the developing world. The fastest growing services subsectors were transport, storage and communications, which are important for Africa's economic development. Broader economic growth and increased export revenue in the past decade, largely due to the commodity boom drove these encouraging trends. Regional trade in services has also increased tremendously especially along the three main lines of finance, telecommunications and retail.

2. *Of the 45 countries where the share of services in output rose, 30 experienced a contraction in manufacturing from the period 2001–2004 to the period 2009–2012*

Many African countries have undergone a process of shifting from agriculture to mainly non-tradable services, without going through a process of manufacturing development marked by significant productivity improvements, formal job creation, exports of sophisticated goods and the application of technology to the wider economy. From the period 2001–2004 to the period 2009–2012, of the 45 countries where the share of services in output rose, 30 experienced a contraction in manufacturing. This suggests that the complementarities between the two sectors are yet to be fully developed in some countries.

3. *Africa's services sector propelled GDP growth in 30 out of 54 countries during 2009–2012*

Weighted real GDP growth rates were calculated for each African country, and the contribution of the services sector to real growth was assessed. This exercise confirmed the importance of services acting as a cushion for the national economy at times of global economic shocks. For the period from 2009 to 2012, the services sector was the most significant driver of economic growth in 30 out of 54 African countries, accounting for more than 50 per cent of real economic growth. It accounted for more than 70 per cent of total real economic growth in 12 countries, of which 7 had services accounting for more than 50 per cent of their GDP.

4. *The share of services in real GDP was highest among manufactures exporters and lowest for fuel exporters*

The share of services in Africa's real output rose from 45.8 per cent to 49.0 per cent from the period 2001–2004 to the period 2009–2012. Within the categories of exports specializations, the shares of services in real output was highest among manufactures exporters (which consist of Lesotho and Tunisia) at 61.7 per cent, followed by services exporters at 57.0 per cent, and was lowest for fuel exporters at 33.9 per cent.

5. *The services sector accounted for 32.4 per cent of total employment in Africa during 2009–2012*

The services sector accounted for 32.4 per cent of total employment in Africa as compared to 56.5 per cent in agriculture and 11.0 per cent in industry during

2009–2012 (International Labour Organization, 2014). Since 2001, the services share of employment has risen steadily while those of manufacturing and agriculture have stagnated. However, countries that are services-oriented do not necessarily source a large share of their formal employment from the services sector. In some countries where the services sector contributed more than 40 per cent to GDP over the period 2009–2012 (e.g. Ethiopia, Mozambique, Rwanda and Zambia), the services sector accounted for less than 20 per cent of total employment. This may be due to the nature of the services sector in these economies and the consequent labour intensity. For the services sector to increase its contribution to employment, the informal sector, which accounts for between 60 to 80 per cent of total employment in Africa, needs to be addressed.

6. *Africa is a marginal player in global services exports and imports – only 11 African countries have consistently been net services exporters since 2005*

Global exports of services in 2012 were $4.4 trillion, and for developing countries they were $1.3 trillion (at current prices). Total imports of services amounted to an estimated $173 billion in 2012 for Africa while exports of services totalled an estimated $98 billion (UNCTADStat, February 2015). In 2012 Africa accounted for only 2.2 per cent of the world's total exports of services compared to 3.6 per cent for developing America, and 24.3 per cent for developing Asia. The continent accounted for 4.0 per cent of total world's services imports compared to 5.2 per cent for developing America and 27.9 per cent for developing Asia. Only 11 African countries have consistently been net services exporters since 2005, 9 of which are dependent on exports of travel (mainly tourism) services. Africa continues to capture a small share of global trade in services because of a lack of strategic support to the sector, hence the need for the continent to build and expand on services trade activities that may generate greater value added.

7. *Foreign bank penetration in terms of both ownership and bank assets is comparatively much higher in Africa than in other regions*

Since the 1990s the ownership structure of African banks has been radically transformed. Foreign bank ownership in Africa has almost doubled since 1995, rising from 120 to 227 banks by 2009. In Africa foreign bank assets as a share of total bank assets in 2009 was 58 per cent; the OECD equivalent was 38 per cent. Since the global financial crisis, there has been a trend in Africa towards both greater cross-border activity and consolidation in the banking sector.

8. *Effective regulatory coordination requires the creation of cross-border supervisory and crisis management groups for systemically important banks in Africa*

Given the rising prevalence of cross-border banking, for Africa's largest cross-border banks countries will need to consider establishing bank-specific supervisory colleges and strengthen national and regional cross-border supervisory practices. This will require improved central bank coordination, resolution frameworks and stronger burden-sharing arrangements. For those countries and banks where systemic cross-border risks are identified, this may also require greater pan-African coordination and monitoring through the Financial Stability Board Regional Consultative Group for Sub-Saharan Africa and the Community of African Banking Supervisors.

9. *Most commitments on financial services in the African schedules translate into limitations or restrictions on ownership and control of investment and employment decisions on foreign banking activity*

While most African countries initiated financial sector liberalization in the context of structural adjustment programmes during the 1980s and 1990s, the liberalization of financial services is now conducted in the context of the GATS. Indeed, financial services represent the third most committed services sector in African GATS schedules, after tourism and business services. A total of 20 African member States have made important commitments that are specific to financial services. Most limitations in Africa pertain to authorization and licensing requirements, as well as limitations on the form, amount or control of the investment of foreign banks mostly in mode 3 and mode 4. These two modes are conduits for investment and employment decisions on foreign banking activity in a given market and can influence the decision of a foreign bank seeking local presence abroad. Hence, they are critical elements that also reflect the level of restrictiveness foreign banking faces in Africa and have influenced the international banking scene taking shape in the continent today.

10. *African countries need to explore the potential for positioning themselves as services suppliers in global and regional value chains in goods and services*

Services are also enablers of many production and sales processes. There are important input–output linkages between manufacturing and services. For example, in South Africa, of all domestically produced intermediate inputs into manufacturing,

31.4 per cent are purchased from the services sector while 18.6 per cent of all domestically sourced intermediate inputs into services come from manufacturing. There is significant scope for African countries to position themselves as reliable and competitive services suppliers in manufacturing value chains. Global value chains can offer significant new opportunities for structural transformation in Africa. About 60 per cent of global trade consists of trade in intermediate goods and services that are incorporated at various stages in the production process of goods and services for final consumption (UNCTAD, 2013a).

C. MAIN MESSAGES AND RECOMMENDATIONS

The policy analysis and discussion underlying this report can be recast in six main messages.

- First, the services sector has the potential to become a significant driver of sustained economic growth and structural transformation in Africa. This would, however, require policies to be aligned to build complementarities between the services sector and other sectors of the economy especially manufacturing. Several services are likely to exert positive spillover effects on other sectors of the economy (e.g. ICT, finance and infrastructure, but also distribution and logistics). Africa must make greater efforts to link these services and industries, that is, to prioritize those services that are relevant for a value chain that is strategically important to a certain country. (For example, Botswana has generated higher benefits from its diamonds industry since it promoted downstream linkages with cutting and polishing activities; similarly the Nigerian oil industry has created some strong upstream linkages with exploration, project and construction services). A precondition for this requires a proactive policy response from African Governments, with measures tailored to support businesses in the services sector and forging public–private partnerships.

- Second, services provision remains suboptimal and is delivered at a high cost. Various regulatory and policy shortcomings prevail, which explain these inefficiencies and impede Africa from fully capitalizing on its services sector potential. For Africa to better harness the potential of its services economy, regulation of and policies for infrastructure services need to better target existing market failures including issues of accessibility, quality, affordability and competition. Indeed, because infrastructure services have a strong bearing on the cost structure of many of Africa's exports, including commodities and manufactures, improving the quality and quantity of such services will enhance the continent's competitiveness. This is all the more important if the continent is to achieve structural transformation.

- Third, for Africa to build on established intra-African trade — which has a more sophisticated composition than its commodity exports to the rest of the world and a higher intensity of services component — the link between human capital and high value added services (i.e. having good software developers, well-trained financial expertise etc.) needs to be better supported. This requires stronger State intervention in developing technical training systems and subsidizing higher education. Without this State support, it will be difficult for most African countries to exploit "knowledge-intensive trade" opportunities and to insert themselves as service suppliers into both higher value global and regional value chains for goods and services.

- The fourth message relates to the regulatory challenges and opportunities of liberalizing services trade. Although African countries have made efforts to address services trade at the national, regional and global levels, a policy disconnect prevails between these three levels, hampering Africa's opportunities to tap into the benefits of greater services trade. Policymakers and negotiators at these three levels need to cooperate and engage to bridge this divide, so that Africa may better harness the gains of greater services trade and market integration.

- The fifth message places emphasis on the potential role of services enhancing existing regional integration efforts and processes. In order to boost the prospective benefits of greater intra-African trade, the CFTA negotiations need to incorporate services trade. The impact of a continent-wide free trade area will only be meaningful for Africa if services are opened up in parallel with trade in goods.

- Finally, recent studies suggest that the informal sector ranges from 50 to 80 per cent of GDP in Africa. It inhibits enterprise development and the continent's services trade potential. Specific measures are required to support the formalization of informal service providers with a view to enhancing their productivity. This can be achieved, for example, through the modernization of transport and logistics value chains by addressing the efficacy and fairness of the tax system, lowering corruption and regulatory burdens, providing small business support services, improving access to credit for small firms and enforcing compliance with regulatory frameworks to improve the efficiency and accountability of public institutions.

In addition to these key messages, the report makes specific policy recommendations on how to better harness Africa's services trade potential and the related developmental, employment and growth benefits. The main policy recommendations are discussed below.

From the non-exhaustive mapping exercise of existing services trade policies in the African continent at the national, regional and global levels, it became apparent that a disconnect between these three levels exist, which needs to be bridged if Africa is to harness the benefits of greater trade in services. The following policy recommendations are aimed at bridging this hiatus in a practical manner:

Make use of multi-stakeholder consultations for policy processes at all levels

African countries have made strides to regulate services trade at the national, regional and global levels. Nonetheless, a policy disconnect prevails between these three levels, hampering Africa's opportunities to tap into the benefits of greater services trade. Policymakers and negotiators at these three levels need to link and engage to bridge this divide, so that Africa may better harness the gains of greater services trade and market integration.

Efforts to align the different levels of policy will require political will, considerable resources and a sensitization and advocacy agenda. African member States and regional economic communities have a number of tools available (such as multi-stakeholder consultation processes, interministerial and parliamentary coordination groups and working parties, focus groups, and surveys) to inform and support these policy processes. This exercise needs to start early on, at a policy design stage which embraces multi-stakeholder approaches and consultation.

Increase efforts to operationalize and implement existing African Union decisions and institutions on trade

National and regional efforts to transpose African Union decisions must be doubled up, as evidence on the ground suggests that part of the disconnect between policies and realities lies in the absence of operationalization and mainstreaming of services trade into existing policy instruments, including monitoring and evaluation. The national mapping of services policies exercise suggests that there is a poor formulation of a services development strategy at both the national and regional economic community levels, which could trump any efforts at the continental level to develop a pan-African strategy for services. In parallel, existing institutions, such as the High-Level African Trade Committee, need to be vested with sufficient resources and autonomy to implement a services trade agenda that is coherent and coordinated at the three policy levels.

Include services trade in any CFTA negotiations strategy

In order to boost the prospective benefits of greater intra-African trade, the CFTA negotiations need to incorporate services trade. The impact of a continent-wide free trade area will only be meaningful for Africa if services are opened up in conjunction with liberalizing trade in goods, especially as many services are critical trade enablers and have the potential to create important backward and forward linkages in the services economy that give rise to employment and growth opportunities.

From the applied case study on the financial sector covered in chapter 5, there are also several policy recommendations that address the financial sector, as this services subsector has evolved rapidly in recent years. As Africa becomes increasingly integrated into global financial markets through foreign banking, there are several potential pitfalls that African policymakers and regulators need to both avoid and consider when exploring opportunities to harness greater capital flows towards improving productive capacity and economic diversification for a transformational agenda in the continent. African policymakers must improve the prudential regulation of the sector.

Address structural impediments to finance

An imperative for realizing the benefits of a prosperous and efficient financial services sector is that Africa tackles critical structural impediments that burden financial sector development, growth and inclusion. These impediments include poor infrastructure, monopolies and inadequate regulation of the sector. Many African member States still need to introduce policies which foster greater domestic competition and address financial market concentration. Greater financial sector diversification and competition through better regulation could also reduce the impact of external shocks. Measures to help banks deal with regulatory hurdles that constrain access to finance might include making more State benefits available electronically and providing official identification cards to make it easier for banks to verify the identity of potential customers, thereby easing access to financial services for the unbanked.

In tackling the chronic undersupply of financial services in rural areas, regulation can also be instrumental to tackle financial market information asymmetries and moral hazard while supporting government efforts to improve financial inclusion, integrity and stability. Major possible reform areas include improving property rights regimes; using the extensive rural branch networks of State and development banks to extend access quickly and relatively cheaply to rural financial services; developing regulatory systems that engender confidence in the role of non-bank financial institutions in rural savings mobilization and as channels for rural payments and transfer of remittances; diversifying the supply of financial products and services in the banking sector; and regionalizing financial markets through legal harmonization and cross-listing at the regional level.

Align regional and multilateral regulatory frameworks for financial services

Africa could also benefit from improved regulation by ensuring there is greater consistency in the regional and multilateral frameworks that already exist for financial services. For example, prudential regulation appears to be overlooked in many African GATS schedules of commitments; this is an area where African countries wishing to regulate the entry of foreign banks should be able to exercise discretion on the basis of their prudential regulation. In addition, countries which are yet to liberalize their financial services sector, have to make sure they use the flexibilities the system has to offer, by inscribing prudential carve-outs as MFN exemptions. The definition of these carve-outs will require greater coordination between trade policymakers and central banks as well as other financial sector authorities and stakeholders.

Furthermore, greater efforts to align the sector with existing regional regulation, such as the protocols covering aspects of financial sector integration and/or investment, such as the Arab Maghreb Union, EAC, ECOWAS and SADC, will be required. As the continent makes greater progress in regional integration, here too, the formulation of carve-outs will be required to cater to financial integration and the emergence of a regional banking sector.

The above-mentioned disconnect is counterproductive especially with respect to regulatory issues and frustrates deeper regional trade. For instance, financial services regulatory frameworks in some countries (e.g. in a regional economic community) are contrary to regional financial services and investment protocols which are supposed to be binding on member States of that regional economic community. A national strategy or plan that incorporates financial services must be aligned to regional plans, as per the country's regional economic community membership, and also to global issues. In addition, these strategies must clearly define services as per the four modes of GATS and also identify embedded and embodied services as a way to properly diagnose and understand the services sectors they deal with or plan for.

D. CONCLUSION

Promoting the integrated treatment of trade, investment, finance and technology for inclusive and sustainable development could be a key sub-theme of the fourteenth session of the United Nations Conference on Trade and Development (UNCTAD XIV). Fostering the contribution to growth, trade and development of services in Africa is one of the key means through which UNCTAD XIV can begin to realize this objective and support regional integration processes in Africa en route to a CFTA. The African Union has committed itself to the creation of a CFTA which encompasses free trade in both goods and services by 2017. This report welcomes the commitment to a CFTA but notes that African countries have not fully reaped the gains from services trade through the GATS and bilateral investment treaties. Furthermore, the report stresses the need for Governments to address a major policy disconnect between national, regional and global levels, which needs to be bridged if Africa is to harness the benefits of greater trade in services. Finally, it stresses that the services sector has the potential to become a significant driver of sustained economic growth and structural transformation in Africa, if effective regulatory frameworks and policies are aligned to build complementarities between the services sector and other sectors of the economy.

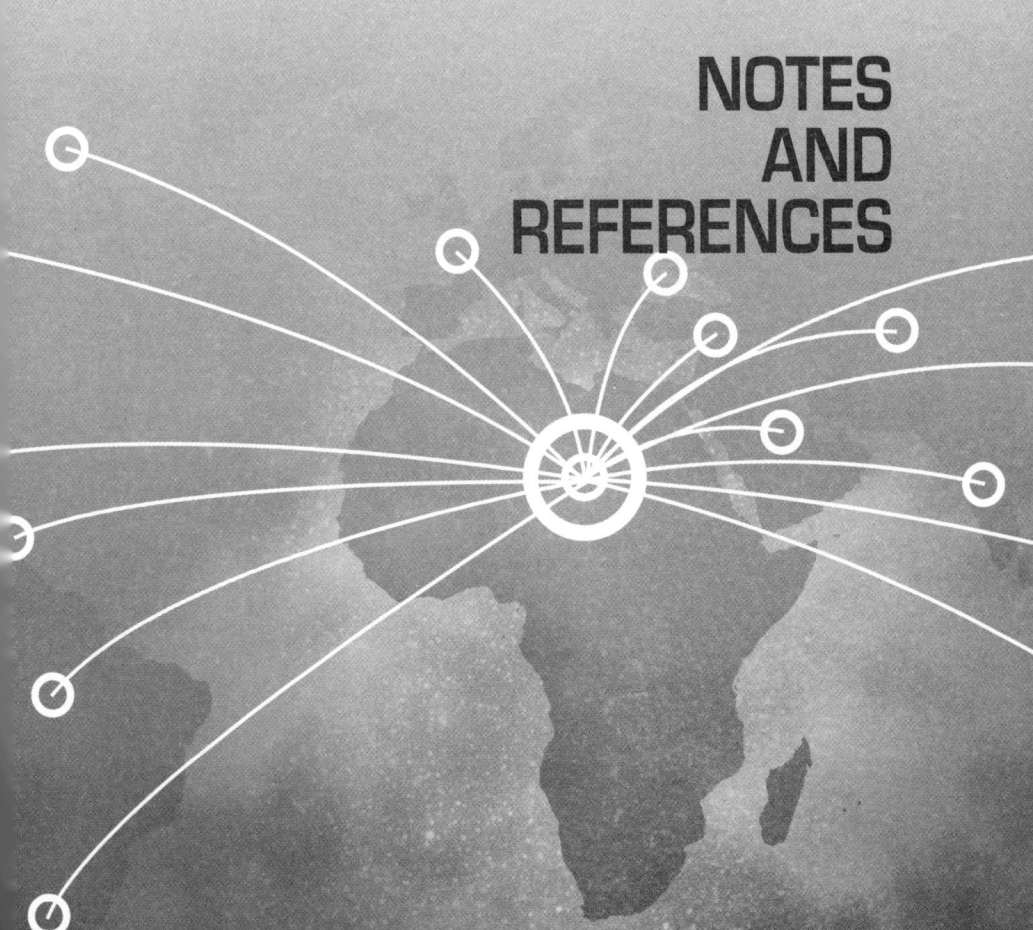

NOTES
AND
REFERENCES

NOTES

1   Total value added is referred to as output in this report and is used as a measure of output instead of GDP to ensure that the shares of the three main economic sectors (services, industry and agriculture, hunting, forestry and fishing) in output add up to 100 per cent. The total may not always be 100 per cent due to discrepancies in the original data and rounding (see notes to table 1).

2   Weighted real GDP growth = (share of services in GDP * real growth in services) + (share of industry in GDP * real growth in industry) + (share of agriculture, hunting, forestry and fishing in GDP * real growth in agriculture, hunting, forestry and fishing). The contribution of services to real growth = (share of services in GDP * real growth in services) / weighted real GDP growth. Figures used are averages for the period 2009–2012. All values are at constant 2005 dollars.

3   The Programme for Infrastructure Development in Africa is a joint initiative of the African Development Bank, the African Union Commission and the Planning and Coordinating Agency of the New Partnership for Africa's Development, in collaboration with several other African stakeholders, including regional economic communities and member States, and provides a common framework to build the infrastructure necessary for more integrated transport, energy, ICT and transboundary water networks, to boost trade and stimulate growth.

4   Regulatory independence may be considered to consist of the following three elements: an arm's-length relationship with regulated firms, consumers and other interests; an arm's-length relationship with political authorities; and the attributes of organizational autonomy (such as dedicated funding and exemptions from restrictive civil service salary rules) necessary to foster the requisite expertise and underpin such relationships.

5   The eight regional economic communities recognized by the African Union are as follows: the Arab Maghreb Union, the Community of Sahel-Saharan States, the Common Market for Eastern and Southern Africa (COMESA), EAC, the Economic Community of Central African States, ECOWAS, the Intergovernmental Authority on Development and SADC.

6   See box 1 on four modes of service delivery.

7   See COMESA, 2014; EAC, 2009; SADC, 2012.

8   Short-term (less than three years), medium-term (three to seven years) and long-term (more than seven years) targets.

9   For a list of GATS schedules of WTO members , see: http://i-tip.wto.org/services/Search.aspx (accessed 5 April 2015)

10 In the political economy of trade negotiations, schedules are a result of a multilateral process cross-sectoral request-offer. For example, a country may have prioritized agricultural negotiations and hence has been more willing to give away services in return for higher protection of its agricultural markets at the moment of entry into WTO. In particular, schedules of countries that joined WTO at a later stage may reflect the high entry costs of the accessions process.

11 A carve-out is an exception (exemption) to a rule or agreement.

12 Beyond the GATS schedules that reflect what each WTO member is committed to offer to the membership, demand-side interests of African members pertain to what is being offered to them (albeit non-exclusively) by the rest of the members in their schedules, as well as through the interpretation of GATS rules (e.g. at Services Council level) and trade ministerial rounds, where the General Council can take decisions that exclusively target Africa.

13 For example, a submission proposed by the Africa Group for services contributed to the adoption of two modalities to govern the treatment of autonomous liberalization and special treatment of LDCs in WTO at Services Council level (WTO, 2003a, 2003b).

14 M2 is money and quasi money comprising the sum of currency outside banks, demand deposits other than those of the central Government, and the time, savings, and foreign currency deposits of resident sectors other than the central Government (World Bank, 2014).

15 Prudential regulation, concerns regulatory monitoring of a bank's asset quality and effectiveness of monitoring; capital adequacy; and other portfolio restrictions to avoid financial instability.

REFERENCES

Acharya VV and Schnabl P (2010). Do global banks spread global imbalances? The case of asset-backed commercial paper during the financial crisis of 2007–09. NBER Working Paper No. 16079. National Bureau of Economic Research, Inc.

African Development Bank (2010). *African Development Report 2010: Ports, Logistics and Trade in Africa.* Oxford University Press, New York.

African Development Bank (2014). Africa Infrastructure Country Diagnostic. Available at http://www.infrastructureafrica.org/tools/data (accessed 13 November 2014).

African Development Bank, OECD Development Centre and United Nations Development Programme (2014). *African Economic Outlook 2014: Global Value Chains and Africa's Industrialization.* OECD Publishing. Paris.

African Development Bank, Organization for Economic Cooperation and Development, United Nations Development Programme, Economic Commission for Africa (2013). *African Economic Outlook 2013: Structural Transformation and Natural Resources.* Organization for Economic Cooperation and Development. Paris.

African Union (2006a). Migration policy framework for Africa. EX.CL/276(IX). Banjul. 25–29 June.

African Union (2006b). Common African position on migration and development. EX.CL/277(IX). Banjul. 25–29 June.

African Union (2014a). Uganda validates the African Union report on higher education services in Uganda. African Union Commission press release. No. 274/2014. 16 October.

African Union (2014b). Burkina Faso validates the report of the African Union on cultural services. African Union Commission press release No. 103/2014. 15 May.

African Union (2014c). Decision on the Report of the High-level African Trade Committee on Trade Issues, Assembly/AU/Dec.531 (XXII).

Aghion P, Fally T and Scarpetta S (2007). Credit constraints as a barrier to the entry and post-entry growth of firms. *Economic Policy*. (22)731–779.

Anderson K and Yao S (2001). How can South Asia and sub-Saharan Africa gain from the next WTO round? No. 3170. Centre for Economic Policy Research.

Bank for International Settlements (2012). Core principles for effective banking supervision. September. Available at http://www.bis.org/publ/bcbs230.htm (accessed 13 April 2015).

Barth JR, Caprio G Jr and Levine R (2013). Bank regulation and supervision in 180 countries from 1999 to 2011. NBER Working Paper No. 18733. National Bureau of Economic Research, Inc.

Baumann U and Nier E (2003). Market discipline and financial stability: Some empirical evidence. *Financial Stability Review*. (14)134–141.

Beck T, Fuchs MJ and Uy M (2009). Finance in Africa: Achievements and challenges. Policy Research Working Paper No. 5020. World Bank.

Beck T, Singer D, Fuchs M and Witte M (2014). Making cross-border banking work for Africa. No. 89202. World Bank.

Beck T, Todorov R and Wagner W (2013). Supervising cross-border banks: Theory, evidence and policy. *Economic Policy*. 28(73):5–44.

Bellmann C (2014). The Bali Agreement: Implications for development and the WTO. *International Development Policy|Revue internationale de politique de développement*. Articles and debates 5.2.

Benjamin N and Mbaye AA (2014). Informality, growth and development in Africa. World Institute for Development Economics Research Working Paper No. 2014/052. United Nations University.

Berg G and Fuchs MJ (2013). Bank financing of SMEs in five sub-Saharan African countries: The role of competition, innovation and the government. Policy Research Working Paper No. 6563. World Bank.

Bleeke J and Ernst D (1991). The way to win in cross-border alliances. *Harvard Business Review*. 69(6):127–35.

Borchert I, Gootiiz B and Mattoo A (2012). Guide to the services trade restrictions database. Policy Research Working Paper. No. WPS6108. World Bank.

Brown AC, Stern J and Tenenbaum B with Gencer D (2006). *Handbook for Evaluating Infrastructure Regulatory Systems*. World Bank. Washington, D.C.

Buch CM, Koch CT and Koetter M (2011). Size, productivity, and international banking. *Journal of International Economics*. 85(2):329–334.

Claessens S and Van Horen N (2014). Foreign banks: Trends and impact. *Journal of Money, Credit and Banking*. 46(s1):295–326.

COMESA (2001). Protocol on the Free Movement of Persons, Labour, Services, Right of Establishment and Residence.

COMESA (2004). Framework for liberalizing trade in services.

COMESA (2014). Report of the thirty-second meeting of the Council of Ministers. CS/CM/XXXII/2. Kinshasa, Democratic Republic of Congo. February.

Demirguc-Kunt A (2006). Finance and economic development: Policy choices for developing countries. Policy Research Working Paper. No. WPS3955. World Bank.

Demirguc-Kunt A and Klapper L (2012). Measuring financial inclusion: The global Findex database. Policy Research Working Paper 6025. World Bank.

Dihel N, Fernandes AM, Mattoo A and Strychacz N (2005). Reform and regional integration of professional services in East Africa. *Economic Premise*. No. 32. World Bank. September.

EAC (2009). Protocol Establishing the EAC Common Market.

Economic Commission for Africa (2013). Sustainable Tourism Master Plan for the Intergovernmental Authority on Development Region: 2013–2023. Available at http://www.uneca.org/publications/sustainable-tourism-master-plan-inter-governmental-authority-development-igad-region (accessed 1 April 2015).

Economic Commission for Africa, African Union and African Development Bank (2010). *Assessing Regional Integration in Africa IV: Enhancing Intra-African Trade*. Economic Commission for Africa. Sales No. E.10.II.K.2. Addis Ababa.

Eberhard A, Rosnes O, Shkaratan M and Vennemo H (2011). *Africa's Power Infrastructure: Investment, Integration, Efficiency*. World Bank. Washington, D.C.

Eichengreen BJ, Mussa M and Dell'Ariccia G (1998). *Capital Account Liberalization: Theoretical and Practical Aspects*. International Monetary Fund. Washington, D.C.

Eifert B, Gelb A and Ramachandran V (2008). The cost of doing business in Africa: Evidence from enterprise survey data. *World Development*. 36(9):1531–1546.

Escribano A, Guasch JL and Pena J (2010). Assessing the impact of infrastructure quality on firm productivity in Africa: Cross-country comparisons based on investment climate surveys from 1999 to 2005. Policy Research Working Paper No. 5191. World Bank.

Estache A and Wodon Q (2014). *Infrastructure and Poverty in Sub-Saharan Africa*. Palgrave Macmillan. New York.

Financial Times (2014a). Ecobank board ousts chief executive Thierry Tanoh. 11 March.

Financial Times (2014b). African banks: Fragile dream. 12 March.

Estache A and Wodon Q (2014). *Infrastructure and Poverty in Sub-Saharan Africa*. Palgrave Macmillan.

Foster V and Briceño-Garmendia C, eds. (2010). *Africa's Infrastructure: A Time for Transformation*. World Bank. Washington, D.C.

Frey L and Volz U (2011). Regional financial integration in sub-Saharan Africa: An empirical examination of its effects on financial market development. Proceedings of the German Development Economics Conference. Berlin. No. 29. Verein für Socialpolitik. Research Committee on Development Economics.

Fry MJ (1995). *Money, Interest, and Banking in Economic Development.* Johns Hopkins University Press. Baltimore, Maryland, United States.

Gassner K and Pushak N (2014). 30 years of British utility regulation: Developing country experience and outlook. *Utilities Policy.* 31:44–51.

Global Parnership for Financial Inclusion (2011). Global Standard-Setting Bodies and Financial Inclusion for the Poor: Toward Proportionate Standards and Guidance. White Paper. Available at http://www.gpfi.org/sites/default/files/documents/CGAP. pdf (accessed 9 April 2015).

Hare PG and Davis JR (2006). Institutions and development: What we (think we) know, what we would like to know. Centre for Economic Reform and Transformation Discussion Paper No. 2006/03. Heriot-Watt University.

Harrison AE, Lin JY and Xu LC (2014). Explaining Africa's (Dis)advantage. *World Development.* 63(C):59–77.

Herrmann K (2012). Uganda: Moving beyond price to recruit international students. Borderless Report. Issue 10. The Observatory on Borderless Higher Education. 19 April.

Infrastructure Consortium for Africa (2013). *Infrastructure Financing Trends in Africa – 2013: ICA Annual Report 2013.* Tunis Belvedere.

International Centre for Trade and Sustainable Development (2014). Africa's largest free trade area set to launch in December. *Bridges Weekly.* 18(36):4–6.

International Labour Organization (2014). Global employment trends database. Available at http://www.ilo.org/empelm/units/employment-trends/lang--en/index. htm (accessed 24 February 2015).

International Monetary Fund (2009). *Balance of Payments and International Investment Position Manual.* Washington, D.C.

IMF (2010). *Balance of Payments and International Investment Position Manual.* International Monetary Fund. Washington DC.

International Monetary Fund (2015). The IMF and the fight against money laundering and the financing of terrorism. 27 March. Available at http://www.imf.org/external/ np/exr/facts/aml.htm (accessed 10 April 2015).

Jack W and Suri T (2011). Mobile money: The economics of M-PESA. National Bureau of Economic Research Working Paper No. 16721. National Bureau of Economic Research, Inc.

Kasekende LA (2010). Developing a sound banking system in sub-Saharan African countries. In: Quintyn M and Verdier G, eds. *African Finance in the 21st Century.* Palgrave Macmillan and the International Monetary Fund. Basingstoke, United Kingdom; New York.

Kessides IN, Noll RG and Benjamin NC (2009). Regionalizing telecommunications reform in West Africa. Policy Research Working Paper No. 5126. World Bank.

Kessie E (2000). Enforceability of the legal provisions relating to special and differential treatment under the WTO agreements. *The Journal of World Intellectual Property.* 3(6):955–975.

Kessie E and Apea Y (2004). Participation of African countries in the multilateral trading system. In: Yussuf AA, ed. *African Yearbook of International Law.* Martinus Nijhoff Publishers. Leiden. 9–66.

Lin JY and Rosenblatt D (2012). Shifting patterns of economic growth and rethinking development. Policy Research Working Paper Series No. 6040. The World Bank.

Mail and Guardian (2014). *Oil, gas play second fiddle to Nigeria's services sector.* 7 April.

Manrique Carpio C and Comas Mir J (2014). The least developed countries services waiver: Any alternative under the GATS? *Goettingen Journal of International Law.* 6:115–143.

Mattoo A and Subramanian A (2003). What would a development-friendly WTO architecture really look like? IMF Working Paper No. 03/153. IMF.

Mavroidis PC (2004). In search of (meaningful) success (the Doha Round). In: *African Yearbook of International Law.* Martinus Nijhoff Publishers. Leiden. 105–120.

Mlachila M, Park SG, Yabara M and the International Monetary Fund. (2013). *Banking in Sub-Saharan Africa: The Macroeconomic Context.* International Monetary Fund. Washington, D.C.

Páez L (2008a). GATS financial services liberalization: How do OECD members' schedules impact commercial banking FDI? *Journal of World Trade.* 42(6):1065–1083.

Páez L (2008b). Regional trade agreements and FDI: Impact of existing RTAs on FDI and trade flows in the Andean Community and implications of a hemispheric RTA in the Americas. *Aussenwirtschaft.* 63(3):1–31.

Páez L (2011). *Liberalizing Financial Services and FDI: Developing a Framework for Commercial Banking FDI.* Palgrave Macmillan. Houndmills, Basingstoke, Hampshire, United Kingdom; New York, United States.

Ploch L and Cook N (2012). Madagascar's political crisis. Report for Congress No. R40448. Congressional Research Service.

Pollitt MG (1997). The impact of liberalization on the performance of the electricity supply industry: An international survey. Journal of Energy Literature. 3:3–31.

Southern African Development Community (2012). Services Trade Protocol.

Schloemann H (2012). The LDC services waiver: Making it work. *Bridges Africa.* 1(4): 13–14.

Stephenson S (2012). Global value chains and services: Implications for African countries. *Bridges Africa.* 1(4):7–9.

Stephenson S and Pfister A-K (2013). The LDC services waiver beyond Bali. *Bridges Africa.* 2(8):27–28.

Stern J and Cubbin J (2005). Regulatory effectiveness : The impact of regulation and regulatory governance arrangements on electricity industry outcomes. Policy Research Working Paper No. 3536. World Bank.

Stern J and Davis JR (1998). Economic reform of the electricity industries of Central and Eastern Europe. *Economics of Transition*. 6(2):427–460.

Stern M and Ward N (2013). Identifying the offensive interests of African Least Developed Countries (LDCs) in WTO Services Negotiations. DNA Economics. 19 February. Available at http://www.ideascentre.ch/wp-content/uploads/2013/10/Offensiveinte restsofAfricanLDCsinWTOserviocesnegotiations-SternandWard1.pdf (accessed 12 April 2015).

Tamirisa NT, Lehmann A and Wieczorek J (2003). International trade in services: Implications for the IMF. IMF Policy Discussion Paper No. 03/6. International Monetary Fund.

Tregenna F (2007). Which sectors can be engines of growth and employment in South Africa? An analysis of manufacturing and services. Presented at the United Nations University World Institute for Development Economics Research Conference on Southern Engines of Global Growth: China, India, Brazil and South Africa. Helsinki. 7 September. Available at http://www.policyinnovations.org/ideas/policy_library/data/engines_of _growth_south_africa/_res/id=sa_File1/growth%20south%20africa.pdf.

UNCTAD (2003). *Challenges and Opportunities for Further Improving the Transit Systems and Economic Development of Landlocked and Transit Developing Countries*. United Nations publication. New York and Geneva.

UNCTAD (2006). Efficient transport and trade facilitation to improve participation by developing countries in international trade. TD/B/COM.3/80. Geneva. 11 December.

UNCTAD (2009). *The Least Developed Countries Report 2009: The State and Development Governance*. United Nations publication. Sales No. E.09.II.D.9. New York and Geneva.

UNCTAD (2011). *Trade and Development Report 2011: Post-Crisis Policy Challenges in the World Economy*. United Nations publication. Sales No. E.11.II.D.3. New York and Geneva.

UNCTAD (2012). *Services, Development and Trade: The Regulatory and Institutional Dimension of Infrastructure Services*. United Nations publication. New York and Geneva.

UNCTAD (2013a). *World Investment Report 2013 – Global Value Chains: Investment and Trade for Development*. United Nations publication. Sales No. E.13.II.D.5. New York and Geneva.

UNCTAD (2013b). *Economic Development in Africa Report 2013: Intra-African Trade – Unlocking Private Sector Dynamism*. United Nations publication. Sales No. E.13. II.D.2. Geneva.

UNCTAD (2014a). *Economic Development in Africa Report 2014: Catalysing Investment for Transformative Growth in Africa*. United Nations publication. Sales No. E.14. II.D.2. New York and Geneva.

UNCTAD (2014b). *Services: New Frontier for Sustainable Development – UNCTAD Findings on Services, Development and Trade*. United Nations publication. New York and Geneva.

UNCTAD (2014c). *UNCTAD Surveys of Infrastructure Regulators and Competition Authorities*. United Nations publication. New York and Geneva.

UNCTAD (2014d). *Services Policy Review Uganda (II)*. United Nations publication. New York and Geneva.

UNCTAD and United Nations Industrial Development Organization (2011). Economic Development in Africa Report 2011: F*ostering Industrial Development in Africa in the New Global Environment*. United Nations publication. Sales No. E.11.II.D.14. New York and Geneva.

United Nations (2009). *System of National Accounts 2008*. Sales No. E.08.XVII.29. New York.

United Nations Capital Development Fund (2006). *Building Inclusive Financial Sectors for Development*. United Nations publication. Sales No. E.06.II.A.3. New York.

Vagliasindi M and Nellis J (2009). Evaluating Africa's experiences with institutional reform for the infrastructure sectors. Africa Infrastructure Country Diagnostic Working Paper No. 23. World Bank.

Visa sub-Saharan Africa (2013). Realizing potential: Connecting Africa. Available at http://www.adriansaville.com/sites/default/files/Visa%20Africa%20Integration%20 Index%20-%20Adrian%20Saville%20and%20Lyal%20White%20-%20Long%20 Pap....pdf (accessed 12 April 2015).

Wakeman-Linn J and Wagh S (2008). Regional financial integration: Its potential contribution to financial sector growth and development in sub-Saharan Africa. Session IV: Beyond banking – Regional financial integration. African Finance for the 21st Century. High-level seminar organized by the IMF Institute in collaboration with the Joint Africa Institute. 4 and 5 March. Tunis.

World Bank (2012). African financial sectors and the European debt crisis: Will trouble blow across the Sahara? Financial Sector Policy Note No. 70434. January. Available at https://openknowledge.worldbank.org/bitstream/handle/10986/12686/704340E SW0P11800Finance0policy0note.pdf?sequence=1 (accessed 12 April 2015).

World Bank (2014a). Data. World development indicators. Available at http://data. worldbank.org/products/wdi (accessed 8 April 2015).

World Bank (2014b). Global Finance Development Database. Available at http://econ. worldbank.org/WBSITE/EXTERNAL/EXTDEC/EXTGLOBALFINREPORT/0,,content MDK:23492070~pagePK:64168182~piPK:64168060~theSitePK:8816097,00.html (accessed 2 Febrary 2015).

World Bank and Global Partnership for Financial Inclusion (2015). Group of 20 financial Inclusion Indicators database. Available at http://datatopics.worldbank.org/ g20fidata/ (accessed 9 April 2015).

World Economic Forum, World Bank and African Development Bank (2009). *The Africa Competitiveness Report 2009*. World Economic Forum. Geneva.

World Trade Organization (2011). Preferential treatment to services and service suppliers of least-developed countries. Decision of 17 December 2011. WT/L/847 December. Available at https://www.wto.org/english/thewto_e/minist_e/min11_e/ official_doc_e.htm.

World Trade Organization (2013). Operationalization of the Waiver Concerning Preferential Treatment to Services and Service Suppliers of Least-Developed Countries. Ministerial Decision of 7 December 2013. World Trade Organization. Bali, Indonesia.

World Trade Organization (2014). Submission by the Delegation of Uganda on behalf of the LDC group: Collective request pursuant to the Bali decision on the operationalization of the waiver concerning preferential treatment to services and services suppliers of least-developed countries. S/C/W/356. 21 July. Available at http://www.chamber.ca/advocacy/canadian-services-coalition/updates/140724_Collective_Request_LDC_Group.pdf (accessed 12 April 2015).

Wren-Lewis L (2014). Utility regulation in Africa: How relevant is the British model? Utilities Policy. 31:203–205.

World Trade Organization (2001). Guidelines for the scheduling of specific commitments under the General Agreement on Trade in Services (GATS). S/K/92. 28 March.

World Trade Organization (2002). Proposal by Kenya, Nigeria, Senegal, Zambia, Cuba, Pakistan and the Dominican Republic, TN/S/W/3. 10 June.

World Trade Organization (2003a). Modalities for the treatment of autonomous liberalization. TN/S/6. 10 March.

World Trade Organization (2003b). Modalities for the special treatment for least-developed country members in the negotiations on trade in services. TN/S/13. 5 September.

Zhang Y, Parker D and Kirkpatrick C (2004). Competition, regulation and privatization of electricity generation in developing countries: Does the sequencing of the reforms matter? Centre on Regulation and Competition Working Paper No. 30599. Institute for Development Policy and Management, University of Manchester.

Zhang KH (2006). Foreign direct investment in China. *Canadian Foreign Policy Journal.* 13(2):35–50.

Economic Development in Africa - Report series:

2000   Capital Flows and Growth in Africa – TD/B/47/4 – UNCTAD/GDS/MDPB/7
Contributors: Yilmaz Akyüz, Kamran Kousari (team leader), Korkut Boratav
(consultant).

2001   Performance, Prospects and Policy Issues – UNCTAD/GDS/AFRICA/1
Contributors: Yilmaz Akyüz, Kamran Kousari (team leader), Korkut Boratav
(consultant).

2002   From Adjustment to Poverty Reduction: What is New? – UNCTAD/GDS/
AFRICA/2
Contributors: Yilmaz Akyüz, Kamran Kousari (team leader), Korkut Boratav
(consultant).

2003   Trade Performance and Commodity Dependence – UNCTAD/GDS/
AFRICA/2003/1
Contributors: Yilmaz Akyüz, Kamran Kousari (team leader), Samuel Gayi.

2004   Debt Sustainability: Oasis or Mirage? – UNCTAD/GDS/AFRICA/2004/1
Contributors: Kamran Kousari (team leader), Samuel Gayi, Bernhard
Gunter (consultant), Phillip Cobbina (research).

2005   Rethinking the Role of Foreign Direct Investment – UNCTAD/GDS/
AFRICA/2005/1
Contributors: Kamran Kousari (team leader), Samuel Gayi, Richard Kozul-
Wright, Phillip Cobbina (research).

2006   Doubling Aid: Making the "Big Push" Work – UNCTAD/GDS/AFRICA/2006/1
Contributors: Kamran Kousari (team leader), Samuel Gayi, Richard Kozul-
Wright, Jane Harrigan (consultant), Victoria Chisala (research).

2007   Reclaiming Policy Space: Domestic Resource Mobilization and
Developmental States – UNCTAD/ALDC/AFRICA/2007
Contributors: Samuel Gayi (team leader), Janvier Nkurunziza, Martin Halle,
Shigehisa Kasahara.

2008   Export Performance Following Trade Liberalization: Some Patterns and
Policy Perspectives - UNCTAD/ALDC/AFRICA/2008
Contributors: Samuel Gayi (team leader), Janvier Nkurunziza, Martin Halle,
Shigehisa Kasahara.

2009   Strengthening Regional Economic Integration for Africa's Development -
        UNCTAD/ALDC/AFRICA/2009
        Contributors: Norbert Lebale (team leader), Janvier Nkurunziza, Martin
        Halle, Shigehisa Kasahara.

2010   South–South Cooperation: Africa and the New Forms of Development
        Partnership - UNCTAD/ALDC/AFRICA/2010
        Contributors: Norbert Lebale (team leader), Patrick Osakwe, Janvier
        Nkurunziza, Martin Halle, Michael Bratt and Adriano Timossi.

2011   Fostering Industrial Development in Africa in the New Global Environment
        - UNCTAD/ALDC/AFRICA/2011
        Contributors: Norbert Lebale (team leader), Patrick Osakwe, Bineswaree
        Bolaky, Milasoa Chérel-Robson and Philipp Neuerburg (UNIDO)

2012   Structural Transformation and Sustainable Development in Africa -
        UNCTAD/ALDC/AFRICA/2012
        Contributors: Charles Gore and Norbert Lebale (team leaders), Patrick
        Osakwe, Bineswaree Bolaky and Marko Sakai.

2013   Intra-African Trade: Unlocking Private Sector Dynamism
        Contributors: Patrick Osakwe (team leader), Janvier Nkurunziza and
        Bineswaree Bolaky.

2014   Catalysing Investment for Transformative Growth in Africa
        Contributors: Patrick Osakwe (team leader), Rashmi Banga and Bineswaree
        Bolaky.